Death to Life

——————— The Story of Jacob Bawa ———————

— Lisa Tuttle

Library of Congress Catalog Number: 2005928933

ISBN: 1-893270-35-1

Printed in the United States of America

Table of Contents

Forward

From 1994 to 2003 Dr. Jacob Bawa served as a visiting professor at Bethel College in Mishawaka, Indiana. During this period he taught courses in education, biblical literature and African culture. He also escourted students on various study abroad programs to the African continent.

Jacob was highly respected by his colleagues at the college and by his students. Jacob and Rose and their family were a wonderful part of the Bethel Community.

When Jacob felt that the time had come for him to return to Nigeria, we released him with much regret.

Since his return to Nigeria, Jacob has again entered into service with both the United Missionary Church of Nigeria and with the Nigerian government.

This book which Lisa Tuttle has so carefully constructed from missionary notes and interviews and from interviews with Jacob and Rose Bawa preserves for future generations the story of a great man. Only eternity will reveal the extent of Jacob's impact on his world and on ours.

Norman Bridges, Ph.D.
President Emeritus
Bethel College

Chapter One

A Son is Born

As Bagudu Bawa accepted the bowl of food his wife had prepared for dinner, he noticed the line of worry creasing the lovely brown skin of her brow. Rather than sitting and eating with him, she continued to move about the hut, driven to straighten and clean the already immaculate space. She had been like this for days, nervous and restless, yet she had not shared her concerns with Bagudu.

"Come eat, Vainamu."

She glanced his way, eyes shadowed with fear. "I am not hungry tonight."

Determined to uncover the source of her concern, he set his bowl down and moved to her side. "You have not been eating well. Tell me what you are worrying about."

Her hands slid to her swollen belly, and she cradled the child she carried inside. "What if this baby is like all the others?" she asked with haunted eyes. "I don't think I can bear to lose another."

Bagudu sighed and drew his wife into his arms. He understood her fears all too well. He had spent many hours in the field wondering what he had done to offend the gods who cursed his children to their deaths before they even had a chance to live. Vainamu had given him seven children, all sons, and each had died at birth. As much as he wanted a child,

Bagudu scarcely dared to hope for a positive outcome. Each child's death wounded him more deeply than the last.

Wanting to comfort his wife, Bagudu put aside his own fears and made a suggestion. "Perhaps we could visit the boka (witchdoctor) tomorrow and ask him how to keep this child from suffering the fate of our other babies."

Vainamu's eyes lit with hope. "Do you think he could help us?"

Bagudu nodded. "It is worth a try."

The next day they called on the witchdoctor and explained their situation.

As the old man listened, he narrowed his eyes and stared into space, appearing to gaze into another realm to divine the answers they sought. "You have not birthed seven sons. You have given birth to the same child seven times. Each time Vainamu becomes pregnant, the same baby comes back to be reborn and die again. You must break the cycle, and the child will live."

The witchdoctor's explanation seemed implausible, but they were desperate for hope. "Tell us what we must do," they asked, grasping for answers.

"As soon as the mother gives birth, bring the baby to me, and I will cut off the child's smallest finger. This will break the curse and allow the child to live."

Bagudu and Vainamu left the boka's hut, skeptical of the old man's advice. They decided to wait for the birth to see what happened. If the child showed signs of distress, they would allow the witchdoctor to chop off its finger, but only as a last resort.

They had no cause to worry. On November 11, 1935, Vainamu gave birth to a strong baby boy. In the male-dominated Kambari (COME buh ree) tribe, boys always were welcomed, but this one was especially exciting. He was a grandson of the chiefmaker, second in command of the tribe.

News spread quickly from one family compound to the next until the two thousand citizens of Salka, Nigeria, bustled around the village, preparing for a celebration. The women ground millet and guinea corn between two stones until they had crushed them into meal. From the meal they would make tuwo, a porridge-like substance, which is a staple in the Kambari diet. As they worked, they gossiped about what the parents might name the baby. Soon enticing aromas drifted on the breeze. Cooking pots full of yams or beans simmered over fires. Some families boiled chicken; others roasted goat meat and made gravy. The men pulled out their stores of palm wine or beer, anticipating a night of drinking. But they would not celebrate for long.

• • •

Eight days after the celebrated birth, Apalu Jamu, Bagudu's sister, crouched outside the mud hut where the men of her family discussed an important issue affecting the village. As she listened, a feeling of dread slithered through her chest and coiled in her belly. Her young nephew's life was in danger.

Apalu did not know if her heart, already heavy with grief, could bear another tragedy. A few days ago, fever had come upon the baby's mother, causing the festive noise in the village to cease. The villagers abandoned their celebration and instead huddled in their huts, whispering about the cause of the illness.

"Someone in the family has angered the spirits. The mother is being punished," they speculated. Before long, a wail pierced the air and the terrible news spread like the field fires during the dry season. Vainamu had died, leaving her eight-day-old son defenseless against the superstitious townspeople.

According to the Kambari people's ancient beliefs, death did not happen naturally. Evil spirits and curses brought death to the village. When a new mother died, her baby was thought to be the bearer of evil. Babies who killed their mothers were either abandoned in a field far from the village or buried alive beside their dead mothers.

As head of the family, the chiefmaker had called upon the boka to ascertain the cause of the mother's death and prescribe a method to counteract the black magic. Apalu had followed behind and now lingered outside the hut listening to their discussion.

The boka stood in the midst of the men. "This child has caused its mother's death." He glanced with disdain at the wiggling infant lying on a mat of woven grass.

The baby stared back with a wide-eyed innocence that defied the accusations made against him.

"The evil upon the infant is strong enough to keep the child alive after its mother died. The baby must die, or it will bring disaster to the family and the village." The witch doctor was insistent. "You must lay the baby beside Vainamu in the grave and bury it alive."

Apalu's knees went weak at the pronouncement. Her sister-in-law's baby buried alive? Unthinkable. Apalu rushed into the hut and gathered the child into her arms, determined to protect him even at the cost of her own life. "You will not bury him alive! I will not allow you. Give him to me, and I will raise him."

The men glared at Apalu. Women were not allowed at the meetings, nor were they permitted to contradict a man, especially a tribal leader or the witch doctor. In arguing for the child's life, Apalu risked bringing severe punishment upon herself.

She searched the crowd for an ally and saw her brother. "Bagudu, he is your son. Do not let them kill him!"

Ravaged by grief, Bagudu did not possess the energy to look up or even speak.

Apalu swallowed hard, realizing she would have to fight this battle alone.

The chiefmaker stared at his daughter, surprised by her uncharacteristic defiance. She had been taught to be obedient and compliant, as were all the Kambari women. But rather than cower from his scowl, Apalu hugged the baby tighter and returned his gaze with determination glinting in her brown eyes.

"We cannot risk bringing the curse upon our village." The old man looked at the floor, thinking of the risks he would face if the child were allowed to live. Crops could wither in the field. Fire might destroy the village. A plague could sweep through the families. The old man grieved his daughter-in-law's death, and he felt reluctant to lose his grandson as well. But he could not justify sparing the life of one child at the risk of the whole village. Yet he wavered in his decision. Though he understood the necessity of ending the curse, he disliked burying a living infant.

He turned to face Apalu. "If you take this baby, you cannot raise him in this community because the whole village would be against us. You would have to move away."

"I will take the child away and live in another village," Apalu agreed, backing toward the door.

"The child will bring the curse on you," someone argued.

"Look at him," she said, staring into the infant's sweet face. "I do not believe this little baby is evil. Let me take him away."

In a moment of compassion, the chiefmaker agreed. "Go, then. You must leave the village before sunset."

• • •

Apalu hurried away from the meeting hut, determined to carry the child to safety before her father changed his mind. But while she had gained her father's permission, she had yet to face her husband. When Jamu returned home from the fields in the evening, he found her packing their possessions.

"What are you doing?"

"We must leave the village," she explained, rolling the grass mats that covered the floor of their hut.

"Why? What has happened?" he asked, confusion and concern rippling across his face. Then he turned and saw the baby sleeping in a calabash (gourd) on one side of the hut. "Why is the baby here?"

"Today I went to my father's compound, and I heard the men talking with the boka. They were going to bury the baby with his mother tomorrow. I could not let that happen. I begged for his life. They gave him to me, but we must leave the village."

Jamu understood the tribe's beliefs and knew why the villagers would not want the child to stay in the community. He had shared Apalu's concern for the child, but to leave the village and all they had worked for ....

"This is our home! We have built a good life here," he argued.

Apalu set aside her work and came to stand before him. Gripping his hands she pleaded her case. "Think, Jamu. We would have a son again." Apalu and Jamu had brought a son into the world years earlier, but lost him to sickness. Since then, they had not been able to conceive. She longed for a child, and in the coming years Jamu would benefit from a son's help in the fields.

"We could go to Busura," she suggested.

Jamu considered this plan. Busura, a Kambari village just six miles north, was known for its excellent farmland. As he thought of the better farming conditions and the crops he could grow, the prospect of moving became more appealing.

"Are you sure you want this, Apalu? We will be leaving our whole family and starting again just for the sake of this baby."

She turned to stare at the sleeping child in her care, her eyes aglow with love. "I am sure."

Jamu saw her determination and knew he could not deny her. "Then we will go."

Chapter Two

Jacob's New Home

The load on Jamu's back grew heavy, and the scorching sun baked his brown skin as he trudged toward their new village. Apalu, carrying the baby in a sling on her back and a stack of calabashes in her arms, looked equally weary.

"We must give the child a name," Jamu said, hoping conversation would distract them from their discomfort. "Have you considered any names?"

"I think we should call him Yakubu (Jacob) Bawa," Apalu answered.

Jamu smiled at his wife. "I like it." The son they had lost years earlier was called Yakubu, and it seemed appropriate to pass on the name. Kambari custom compelled them to give him the Bawa, meaning "servant." A child who lives after the death of its siblings is named Bawa, or servant, because the child is expected to serve others, compensating for the absence of the dead children.

The six-mile walk from Salka to Busura seemed much longer due to the weight of the loads they carried, but they finally arrived in their new village.

In 1935, the members of the Kambari tribe of Nigeria existed much as they had for centuries. The land provided all they needed for survival. They made their huts from the earth, mixing water and soil until they formed a thick mud, good for building walls. The sun and heat dried the mud into a sturdy brick-like substance that lasted years and needed little repair. The long grasses from nearby fields formed an excellent rooftop covering when bundled and laid across the roof's bamboo framework. Most of the men farmed the land and walked to their fields outside the village each day to work. During the dry season from January to March, the crops did not grow, so the men of the village went on an extended hunt. They brought home enough meat to last throughout the year.

Families built their huts in close clusters, called compounds, in order to share the workload and care for one another. A wall of woven grasses plastered with mud surrounded each family's compound. An entrance hut provided access to the compound. Several large families lived together in a central village. Although Apalu had left her family behind, the other aspects in her life continued much as they had before the move.

While Apalu and Jamu worked to build a new life, they found that taking on the responsibility of raising an orphaned infant came with many difficulties. Feeding the baby was the first and most urgent dilemma. Apalu could not nurse tiny Jacob, so she went from one house to another carrying him in a calabash lined with black fabric, which signified his orphaned status.

"Is there a nursing mother here?" she asked at each door. Whenever she found a nursing woman, she begged her to nurse baby Jacob so he would have some nourishment.

After several weeks, this arrangement grew time-consuming and costly, as Apalu was often expected to pay the women for their nursemaid services. When feeding Jacob began to drain their resources, she decided to visit the tribe's medicine man to see if he could help her. The medicine man was knowledgeable about the healing properties of plants and herbs and could effectively treat many of the Kambari's illnesses and ailments with his natural remedies.

When he saw the baby in the black-lined calabash, the medicine man guessed Apalu's request. Orphaned babies were difficult to feed, and he had helped other adoptive parents on previous occasions.

Apalu showed him the baby and explained that he was barely receiving enough nourishment to survive. "I must find a better way to feed him. I cannot depend on strangers to nurse him."

The medicine man nodded. "I will help you. Come tomorrow, and I will have something for you."

After Apalu left, the medicine man went into the bush and returned with some herbs, which he made into a potion. When Apalu returned the next day, he offered her the herbs. "Drink this, and soon you will be able to feed the baby yourself." Apalu did as he asked, and within days her breasts filled with milk. From then on, she was able to nurse the child.

In addition to feeding and caring for baby Jacob, Apalu gave him his tribal markings. Many of the Nigerian tribes carve lines into the skin on their faces, arms or torsos, forming scars that identify them as members of a certain tribe and village. The tradition dates back to the days when slavers frequently raided Nigeria, carting thousands away from their homes and families. The markings made it easier for slaves who escaped their masters to find their way home to their villages and families.

About ten days after his birth, Apalu used a knife to cut a long marking on each of Jacob's cheeks, beginning beside his nose and extending outward beneath his cheekbones. These lines identified him as a Kambari. He also received several small marks to the right of his mouth, the sign of his family. Apalu rubbed shea butter, a substance similar in texture to olive oil, on the markings to prevent an infection. Made from shea nuts, the butter possessed medicinal qualities. Apalu was satisfied with the scars that formed. If he were ever kidnapped or lost, Jacob could find his way back to her.

• • •

From an early age, Apalu and her husband taught Jacob to follow their pagan belief system, which involved the worship of various gods and the Magiro fetish. They considered this an important responsibility because they wanted Jacob to be religious.

The Kambari believed in a Supreme Being, whom they called the "biggest God." However, the villagers built miniature huts in various places around the village to house more than ten "little gods." They sacrificed chickens and left offerings of food near these knee-high huts, hoping to gain favors from the god who inhabited the dwelling. These little gods were thought to protect the village and its families from evil.

Each village also contained a special mud hut referred to as the fetish hut. Built in a grove of thick trees, shadows and darkness always shrouded the fetish hut. The "bigger god," called Magiro, occupied this mud hut designated for him. Magiro was supposedly a dragon-like being that served as intermediary between the little gods and the biggest God. The Magiro fetish was a male-dominated religion. The men performed the rituals and communicated with the god. The women only obeyed the orders given them, which usually included preparation of food and beer to present as offerings. The women also were required to sacrifice a chicken when the fetish leader called certain festivals.

From time to time, usually when the fetish leader wanted to call a festival, the Magiro would come out of his hut and walk the streets of the village. Heavy footsteps, which sounded suspiciously like the beating of a large drum, preceded his strolls through town. The Magiro often talked to the people in the evenings or when he walked the streets. In reality, a man in the fetish hut talking into a long hollow stick with a whistle-like contraption at the end created the spirit's screechy voice. The fetish leader would interpret the strange noises, serving as mouthpiece for the demon-god.

But the women were ignorant of the great ruse taking place in the village. From birth, the girls were taught that if they looked at the fetish dragon or allowed the fetish dragon to see them, they would die within a matter of days. The women feared Magiro and hid in their huts the instant they heard his drumbeat footsteps or his whistling voice.

Children were told that the dragon would swallow them if he caught them in the streets, so they also ran and hid when they heard his voice or his heavy footsteps sounding through the village streets. Beyond obedience and fear, the women did not participate in the worship or show any spiritual interest. They believed if their husbands faithfully followed the fetish, they would be included in the final reward.

From an early age, Jacob learned the rituals and practices surrounding the worship of the bigger god Magiro. His uncle taught him, "Each time you come to worship, the first thing you do is kill a chicken and smear the blood on the doorpost on the entrance of the mud hut."

As Jacob grew, he began to question the practice. "Why do we have to do this?"

In explanation, his aunt and uncle told him this story: "There is one God that is considered to be the biggest God. The biggest God used to be very close to human beings. Each time you needed food, all you had to do was stretch your hand upward and ask Him, and the God of heaven would give you food. If you needed something else, all you had to do was ask. He was very close. You could even touch Him and feel Him.

"But," they said, "something bad happened. One day a married couple had a misunderstanding. The husband and wife began to argue and fight. The wife grabbed a big, long stick and lifted it up over her head, preparing to hit her husband in anger. As she lifted the stick high, she accidentally poked the right eye of the biggest God, so He flew away. This is why He is no longer close to us today."

They concluded by saying, "We have this problem simply because women caused it. Now we have to go through the bigger god to reach the biggest God."

"So what do I need to do?" Jacob asked.

"Just keep killing the chickens and sprinkling the blood. By keeping the fetish practices, you are pleasing the gods."

Once a year the village came together as a community, and each person was expected to bring an offering of money. The children brought a penny, and each adult offered a shilling, which equaled ten or twelve cents. After collecting the money, the leader traveled into town and purchased a black he-goat. He brought the goat before the people in a community ceremony. The leader placed his hands upon it and said, "We made mistakes all along, and we want you to forgive us our mistakes." Jacob later noted that the chief never asked forgiveness for the tribe's sins, only their mistakes, as if their offenses were purely unintentional.

After the prayer, the chief took an amount of money from the offering and put it into a black bag, which he tied around the goat's neck. Then, four strong young men carried the goat into the wilderness. The goat could not be pulled or dragged. They had to carry it because it served as a holy messenger to God.

They left the animal in a field far from the village, believing the black bag of money would help the goat become a spirit and ascend to heaven. Once in heaven, the goat took the money to the biggest God and gave it to Him as an offering. The goat would remain with the biggest God for about a month before he returned to the earth.

When the goat finally reappeared in or around the village, the people celebrated and rejoiced. They believed the goat returned from heaven with blessings, such as good rains and plentiful crops that year. The men told their wives, "The goat is back from heaven. God said you are to prepare him the best meal. Once you have it ready, we men will take it to the big fetish hut. Men are the ones to take the good food. You can cook it, but do not touch it or taste it, or the bigger god will not answer our prayers."

After the women had worked hard to prepare food and beer, the men took the offering to the big hut and served it to Magiro. If the women had realized that the men were sitting in Magiro's hut and eating the food their wives had prepared, they might have been angered. Because the women were not aware of the deception, they gladly prepared food and sent their husband to perform the fetish rituals.

Children stayed with their mothers while the men practiced this fetish ritual, but at age seven, young boys were initiated into the fetish and taught the secrets of the Magiro. A father made an offering of a goat or other animal to the fetish leader and requested that the men allow his son to participate in the rituals. The men of the tribe then took the young boy to the fetish hut and showed him the drum used to make the sound of Magiro's footsteps, the long, hollow tube that produced Magiro's voice, and the metal rings the men jangled to make the women think Magiro wore bracelets on his ankles.

These revelations often brought a great sense of disappointment to the initiated boys. This great dragon-god they had faithfully served and feared was nothing more than their older brothers and uncles playing tricks on the women. Their religious practices gave the men a clever excuse to sit in the fetish hut, eating the food and drinking the beer they had ordered their wives to make for a god that did not exist. The fetish leaders knew the disappointment. They also had experienced the initiation ceremony and had felt the disillusionment of discovering there was no dragon.

In order to keep the men and boys faithful, they concocted a story. "We know you expected to see a dragon when you came in here. The dragon that watches over the town is a spirit we cannot see. It tells us what to do and gives orders through the mouthpiece (fetish leader), and we must obey." The ceremony concluded with all the men and boys in the village threatening harm to the young boy should he tell his mother the truth about Magiro. Only when he had been sufficiently frightened into silence was he allowed to leave the hut.

Jacob went through his initiation rite around age seven. His uncle and the Magiro elders took him to Magiro's hut in the village. After they showed him the flute and the drums, they seated him in the middle of the room and began the process of intimidation.

"We have been instructed by Magiro to do these things. So do not tell the women what goes on in here or we will get you," one man threatened.

"Don't say anything!" another ordered as he slapped Jacob across the face several times.

The men continued to threaten Jacob for a long time, delivering a few more blows to help make their point. Scared to tears, Jacob agreed to every demand and swore to keep quiet about the secrets he had learned.

So Jacob joined the Magiro fetish, but he did not feel the inner peace and joy he craved when he performed the rituals and served the bigger god. Even at his tender age, he longed for a real spiritual experience, as did many of the Kambari.

• • •

Jacob showed a remarkable ability to learn, even in the primitive setting of his village. Nigeria is home to more than 420 separate tribes, each with its own distinct language or dialect. Since the tribes often interacted, many people in the region were multilingual. By age seven, Jacob spoke three languages: Kambari, Hausa and Fulani. He grew up speaking the Kambari tongue with his aunt and uncle. Hausa, the trade language, was commonly spoken among the tribes and used to barter and sell. He learned Fulani, the language spoken by a nomadic tribe, from playing with Fulani children who frequented the village. Nigeria's educational system did not extend to the many remote tribes and villages, so Jacob did not have access to formal education in his early years. But for the time being, life itself was education enough.

Like all Kambari boys, Jacob worked in the fields with his uncle from the time he was able. The farming season began in April when the rains came to Salka and Busura. The growing season extended through the December harvest. Jamu grew a variety of crops: corn, guinea corn, millet, ground nuts (peanuts), and cotton. As a young adolescent, Jacob was too small for the hard labor required in the field, but he fetched water, ran errands, and performed small tasks to help his uncle.

Apalu sometimes accompanied her husband and adopted child to the field. During planting, harvest, and times when extra hands were needed, she helped with the farming. But her main job involved tending cattle and sheep. She bought and raised the animals to provide extra income for the family. Apalu and Jamu provided well for the family and loved Jacob as their own. They had a good life, but events were brewing that would soon disrupt their happy home.

3

Chapter Three

A Door of Opportunity

When Jacob was seven years of age, some Nigerian government leaders summoned Jacob's grandfather to the emir's palace forty-four miles away from Salka in a village called Kontagora. The emir, also called the paramount chief, ruled over a large segment of Kambari in much the same way a governor leads a state. "It has not been mandatory for you to send children to school, but the laws have changed," the emir explained. "Now you are required to send one child from each family compound to the government school. Because of your important position in the tribe, you must set an example and send one child from your household."

Before that day, the Kambari had resisted sending their children to the schools set up by the British, who ruled the country at that time. The tribes in the rural regions of Nigeria had little use for the white man's ideas about education. The Kambari were mostly farmers, like their fathers and grandfathers before them. They expected their children to follow in the tribal traditions. Schooling would not grow crops or put food on the table.

However, Jacob's grandfather recognized times were changing and the tribe would have to comply with the new laws. "I will go home and talk with the men of my family and decide which children we should send to school."

The old Kambari chiefmaker returned to his family's compound and called the men of each household together. According to Kambari custom, the men first discussed the issue before passing on the information to the women.

The men came in from the fields and gathered in the central meeting building, seating themselves on woven grass mats.

When they had settled and the older man had gained everyone's attention, he began. "The government now requires that each of the five families in our tribe send one child to Auna. The law demands that we obey, so one of you must give up your son. Who will it be?"

A heavy silence settled over the room as the men pondered this unpleasant news. They sat with eyes downcast, refusing to look at the chiefmaker for fear he would think they were volunteering their sons for this dangerous mission.

"Who will it be?" the leader asked again. "One boy must go."

Another long silence passed, then one man spoke up. "Let us go home and discuss this matter with our wives. Let us ask our women if they will give up a child."

The chiefmaker thought a moment and agreed to the suggestion. "Yes. Go and ask your wives. Come again tomorrow, and we will decide which boy to send to the school in Auna."

The men rose and left the hut in haste. That night, the village huts filled with passionate discussions between husbands and wives.

"The tribal leaders said each family in the village must send one boy to the school in Auna. The government demands it," one man told his wife.

Her eyes grew large and round with fear. She pulled her children to her sides and draped strong arms around them protectively. "They will not take my son," she argued vehemently.

When her husband did not rush to agree with her, she continued the debate. "The road to Auna is long and dangerous. He could be captured or killed by robbers."

The man did not argue, for his wife spoke the truth. Traveling between villages often proved hazardous since robbers and thugs could easily ambush travelers on unpopulated stretches of road.

"And even if he does make it safely to the school, I do not trust the men who run the school. They will make him their slave or kill him. I will not risk my son's life!"

The man realized he could not argue with his wife, and in truth, he did not want to argue. Sons were valued in the tribe. They helped in the fields, hunted with the men and shared in the fetish worship. They provided leadership to the family units and represented a tribe's strength in times of war.

The men returned to the meeting hut the next day, each hoping another man would volunteer his child. But no tribe member would relinquish a son.

"But the government demands we send a child," the chiefmaker insisted, his patience growing short. The village could not afford to antagonize the emir and his regime.

The men shrugged helplessly. "Not one mother will part with her child. The dangers are too great. We cannot risk it."

The chiefmaker stared at the men of his family with agitation. "We have no choice. The government demands we send a child. If we do not comply, they will send the police to take our children by force, and we will fall out of favor with the government. We cannot afford that!"

After a long silence, a man spoke up and offered a solution. "We do not want to upset the mothers in our tribe. However, we have concluded that all you need to do is send word to Busura and order Jacob Bawa to go to Auna. He is part of our village and has no mother to grieve if he is enslaved or killed. The government will be appeased, and our wives will not lose a valued son."

Jacob's grandfather considered the man's words and saw the wisdom in the suggestion. For seven years he had worried about the decision to allow Jacob to live when the baby should have been put to death. The old man still worried that the curse might come back upon the family or village and they would suffer for disobeying the beliefs that had governed their tribe for centuries. Perhaps sending Jacob to the school would accomplish what the tribe had failed to do many years earlier—end Jacob's life.

"Yes," he said, seeing the answer to two of his problems. "I will send word to my daughter, Apalu. She cannot refuse if I order her to send the boy. Your children will be spared."

The Kambari men breathed sighs of relief and sent smiles of congratulations around the hut. No one cared about little Jacob Bawa. They all knew the village would be better off if that boy were dead.

• • •

The next week, the chiefmaker sent a messenger to Busura to inform Apalu that she must send Jacob back to Salka. Apalu stared at the messenger with surprise and more than a little suspicion when he relayed her father's instructions. "I am to take the child back to Salka. His grandfather wants him to come home."

Fear flared in her breast. Why would her father ask Jacob to return? "But he has shown no interest in the boy all these years. Why does he want Jacob now?"

"I don't know," the messenger lied. "He did not tell me. I only know they insist I bring him home to Salka."

Apalu realized she could not dissuade the messenger from taking her child away. Rather than relinquish Jacob to the man without any explanation, she decided to accompany them back to Salka and demand answers from her father.

After a long, anxious walk, Apalu arrived at the big compound and immediately sought out her father. When he granted her an audience, she addressed her concerns. "Why have you sent a messenger to take my child from me? What do you want with Jacob?"

He stared at her, his face hard and cold like a mask of stone. "The government demands we send one child to school. We have chosen to send Jacob to Auna."

She dropped to her knees and let out a keening wail. She cried and begged and pleaded with her father not to take her child, but to no avail. The chief would not be swayed. The news devastated Apalu, and she retreated to a hut in her family's compound to grieve.

The day of Jacob's departure arrived too soon. Because she sincerely feared for his life, Apalu refused to relinquish her adopted son. She packed her few possessions, and accompanied Jacob to the edge of the city where he was to meet a police officer assigned to escort him to Auna. If she could not keep him home, she would travel with him to the boarding school.

"Where are you going?" Apalu's cousin asked when she saw the load on Apalu's back.

"I am going with Jacob."

"You cannot go all the way to Auna with him!"

"I can and I will." Apalu raised her chin in defiance, refusing to be swayed.

"Haven't you learned anything, Apalu? He is a cursed child. He can only bring you heartache," her cousin said.

"He is my son now, and I love him. I will not let them take him from me. If he must go, then I will too."

Though many tried to discourage her, Apalu refused to allow Jacob to leave her side. Apalu, Jacob, a policeman and four children from other Kambari compounds started early one morning and walked the twenty-two miles from Salka to Auna, arriving at nightfall. The city, larger than their hometown and full of strange sights and sounds, intimidated Jacob and Apalu. As they walked the dark streets, uncertainty weighed heavily on their hearts. The school would bring changes to their lives that neither felt ready to face.

Jacob had relatives living in Auna, so he and Apalu went to their hut and stayed with their family members that night. As Apalu lay in bed, she hoped that Jacob could live with this family while he attended the school. Knowing he was under the care of relatives would greatly reduce her fears for his safety. The relatives were agreeable to caring for Jacob if arrangements could be made with the school. Early the next morning, Jacob and Apalu made their way to the school. When they arrived, they were ushered into the principal's office. Jacob addressed the man. "My name is Jacob Bawa of the Kambari tribe in Salka. I was asked to come to your school."

"Yes," the man answered. "But who is this lady with you?"

Apalu answered for Jacob. "I am his mother."

The man frowned. "You shouldn't be here."

"Oh, yes, I am supposed to be here," she argued.

"Why?"

"Because my son is here. I am going to be here with him. Even if it means death, I am ready to die," she stated with vehemence.

The principal had no patience for this stubborn woman who was interfering in the usual practices of his school. He ordered one of his staff to call the police. A short time later, a local policeman came, escorted Apalu out and walked her all the way back to the village of Busura to ensure she would not turn around and sneak back to the school to harass the principal.

Apalu cried all the way home, thinking she would never see her precious son again. They had informed her Jacob would live in the school dorms, not with relatives as she had hoped. Even worse, they refused to allow her to visit. Her father's cruelty had ripped her only child from her arms and made him a prisoner to the government's wishes.

Jacob also suffered during the separation. For many weeks, he cried himself to sleep at night, homesick for the only mother he had ever known. Thankfully, the school's schedule included several breaks each year. During these vacations, administrators allowed students to return home to visit family, so Jacob saw Apalu several times a year.

• • •

Soon after Jacob began classes, he was introduced to many changes, including new religious beliefs.

The principal said to him, "You have come to us as a pagan, but this is a Muslim school. We expect all our students to become Muslims."

"What does that mean?" Jacob asked.

"It means you have to believe in Allah and Mohammed his prophet."

Jacob understood these terms because several Muslims lived in the village where he had been raised.

"You will meet an Islamic teacher on Friday, and he will give you a special bath. After that, he is going to do some other things that will introduce you to the Islamic religion."

Jacob wondered about these strange requirements. "Why do I need a special bath? What for?"

"Without going through the ceremony, you can't be confirmed or called a Muslim," his teacher explained.

The principal assured Jacob he needed to take this important step, so he agreed to the ceremony. On Friday, the school officials brought a mallam (teacher) to the school, and Jacob went through the absolution rites. Afterward, Jacob began learning Arabic and reading the Koran as part of his school lessons. Islamic Religious Teaching was a required subject in all public schools. During his years in Auna, Jacob became proficient in reading and writing Arabic as he studied the Koran and memorized verses and passages from the Islamic holy book.

In addition to religious studies, the school's curriculum included history, science, math, geography, and other subjects common to a primary school. Though classes were conducted in the Hausa language, Jacob also studied some English, the official language of Nigeria.

Jacob excelled in his English studies. Midway through one semester the district officer, a British man in charge of the schools in that county, came to the school and sponsored a spelling competition. "As I read a list of English words, you do your best to write them," the officer explained, "and whoever performs the task with 100 percent accuracy will receive a prize." The man showed them the paper-wrapped parcel he carried.

When they had finished, the officer quickly graded the tests and stood before the class to announce the winner. "Jacob Bawa, you received a perfect score. Please step forward and accept your prize." The district officer presented Jacob with the package and congratulations. Jacob returned to his room and opened the prize, excited to find a container full of sugar packets—quite a luxury for a young boy in the 1940s! That accomplishment gave him a sense of satisfaction and a desire to excel in all his studies.

• • •

Jacob had many new experiences living so far away from home. Upon first arriving in Auna, he saw people who looked very different than his Kambari tribesmen. Some had different markings on their faces; some wore different clothes. A few had a different skin color than any people Jacob had seen.

For a boy accustomed to a primitive life in the bush, the sights around town proved entertaining and educational. During one visit to the marketplace, a man walked through the streets, leading a tall, lanky beast with brown fur covering its body.

"What is that?" Jacob asked his friend.

"A camel," the other student explained.

"I have never seen an animal like this." He continued to gape with fascination.

The city market also provided entertainment. Open-bed cargo trucks, or lorries as the British in Nigeria called them, visited the market each day to drop off and pick up loads of food and other goods carried in and out of the cities. Jacob had never seen a vehicle so large and so loud. A few people rode motorcycles in the bush, and on rare occasions, he had seen a car or truck. But these large vehicles were a new and interesting sight.

The buildings in the city were constructed differently than the mud huts of Salka, using large cement bricks to form the walls and sheets of tin on the roof. Jacob had never seen a dormitory before he moved into the school's facilities. Even books were unfamiliar to him. Because the Kambari were largely illiterate, the people of his village had no need for books or reading material.

Through school-organized activities, Jacob discovered engaging pastimes. In order to keep the schoolboys busy and out of trouble, the teachers planned activities from morning until sundown. After school, the boys were required to help with chores and often worked in the school garden. But some evenings and weekends, the teachers encouraged the boys to put aside schoolwork and chores and participate on a sports team. Soccer, also known as football in that country, was one of Jacob's favorite sports. He loved the energy and the competition and always had a good time playing in the games.

Though he still missed his aunt and home, he adapted to his new life at the school and began to appreciate the opportunity given him. Learning to read and write opened a new realm of knowledge to Jacob. He learned about the world and studied different places and cultures that he might not have known about otherwise. The more he learned, the more his hunger for knowledge grew, fueling his desire to continue his education.

Nigeria's underdeveloped educational system could not accommodate every student who wished to enroll in school. Because of the limited space, a student who wished to go on to middle school had to earn the right by scoring high on the national entrance exam. Only those who passed the difficult test could continue their education. After completing his primary education in the government school, Jacob sat for the exam. When the test results came back, Jacob was one of three boys with scores high enough to proceed. He received an invitation to attend a middle school and looked forward to continuing his education after the year-end break.

Attending the government school had initially seemed like a curse, but eventually Jacob saw his education in a boarding school as a blessing. A large, fascinating world lay beyond his primitive hometown, and Jacob relished learning about it. Jacob enjoyed his studies so much he thought he might like to become a teacher some day. With a teaching degree, he could return to Salka and help educate the Kambari children so they, too, could know more about the world beyond the village.

4

Chapter Four

The Good News

With the semester complete and tests finished, Jacob packed his bags and returned to Salka to visit his family until the new semester began. The people of Salka had almost forgotten about the curse surrounding Jacob's birth and had grudgingly accepted him. Even Bagudu tolerated Jacob's visits and showed mild appreciation when Jacob offered to help in the fields while he was home on breaks. Now a teenager, Jacob had grown into a strong young man and an able farm hand.

During this visit to Salka, Jacob's real father, Bagudu, asked to meet with him. "I have not been feeling well, and I am having trouble doing all the farming alone," he explained. "I need you to stay home and help me. You will not return to the school."

Disappointment sliced through Jacob's chest, severing his dreams of becoming a teacher. Part of him wanted to rebel. Bagudu had abandoned Jacob days after his birth. What right did he have to assert his parental authority now? Yet, Jacob could not bring himself to deny his father's request.

Putting aside his own desires, Jacob honored his father's wishes and withdrew from school. While this change in plans caused some sadness, it also brought joy. During Jacob's years away, his aunt Apalu had suffered a terrible loss. Shortly after relinquishing her adopted son to the men at the boarding school, her husband Jamu fell ill and passed away. Alone in Busura with no child, husband, or family to keep her company, she looked forward to visiting with Jacob during his breaks. So when she heard Jacob would remain in Salka at his father's home, Apalu packed her possessions and returned to Salka to live with her family. Jacob and his aunt were reunited.

• • •

Jacob adjusted to living in Salka, trading books and classrooms for a hoe and days spent in the field under the warm Nigerian sun. He formed friendships with the boys his age and settled into village life.

One day, Indazo, a young Kambari boy about Jacob's age, met Jacob in the field and began to talk about a new experience. He carried a small book, which he showed to Jacob. Indazo opened the cover and let Jacob see the first page, a black paper void of text. The next page was red, then white and finally green. Indazo then explained the significance of the colors.

"The black is for sin and darkness which inhabits every man's heart. The red stands for blood which washes away sin, like the goat the elders sacrifice each year, only better. Listen to this verse I learned from the a book the missionaries call the Bible: 'For God so loved the world, that he gave his only begotten Son, that whosoever believeth in him should not perish, but have everlasting life.' God's son shed his blood for my sin so I no longer need to depend on the blood of the goat. Just asking forgiveness washes away my sin and makes me white like this page here." He pointed to the blank white page in his book.

"Now, my heart feels like the green fields in the spring, full of life and growing. All because of Jesus Christ."

"I have not heard about this Jesus or the book you speak of," Jacob replied. "Does it say anything about the Kambari?"

"Yes, it says God loves the whole world, including the Kambari," Indazo explained. "I came to realize this after the missionaries told me about the Lord Jesus Christ. I accepted it, and I believed in the Lord Jesus. I am now a happy person." The joy shining from Indazo's face confirmed his words. "The person who told me about Jesus also taught me that after you become a Christian, you should go out and share the good news with others. I thought since we have been good friends, why don't I begin with you?" Indazo went on to share the gospel of Jesus Christ with Jacob, explaining the way of salvation.

Then Jacob asked Indazo, "How did you hear about this Jesus way? Who told you?"

"You know we have missionaries living in that compound." Indazo pointed to the hut where Art and Gladys Reifel lived.

"Missionaries?" Jacob did not even understand the meaning of the word.

"Bature," Indazo explained. White people. "They told me about Christ, and I became a Christian. I am happy now, and I want to share the gospel. I want you to know that Jesus died for everyone. If the Magiro fetish and our forefathers' beliefs were true, I would not have become a Christian. But I discovered there is no truth in the Kambari idol worship."

Jacob listened intently to all Indazo had to say, interested in this religion that caused his friend to speak with such passion.

Indazo concluded with an invitation. "The missionaries are having a service in a few days. Would you like to go with me?"

Jacob wanted to attend and hear more about the way of Jesus, but he remembered a conversation he had with his father shortly after returning from the government school in Auna.

Bagudu had taken him aside, his face serious and firm. "I realize that you became a Muslim at the school. Now that you are here with me, I want you to forget about the Islamic faith. Our family worships Magiro, and you will too. I do not want you to go into any other religion."

"Other religion? What do you mean?" Jacob asked.

Bagudu shook his head, frustrated. "There are white people in this community trying to influence our children to become Christians. They are trying to take our young people into a white man's religion."

Jacob asked his father, "How do you know it is only a white man's religion?"

"That's what they told me," his father replied.

"Who told you?" Jacob pressed.

"The Muslims that are living here. They told me that Christianity is a white man's religion."

"Did you believe them?" Jacob asked.

"I don't know, but that is what they told me."

But after Indazo explained this Christian religion in clear terms, Jacob knew that faith was not just for white men. Defying his father's edict,

31

Jacob sneaked away from his father's hut and went to the service.

When Jacob walked into the Salka church, he recognized this place of worship was different than any he had experienced before that day. As he watched the believers singing hymns, he saw something different in them. Their faces were shining with a joy unlike any he had witnessed previously. They were truly happy people.

The worshippers sang a hymn that touched Jacob's heart. "Jesus loves me, this I know, for the Bible tells me so. Little ones to him belong. They are weak but he is strong."

The words affected Jacob deeply. He was a young man, searching for a true way. As he listened, God spoke to his heart, telling Jacob he needed Jesus as his personal Savior.

After the song ended, a gray-haired missionary woman Jacob would later come to know as Isabelle Hollenbeck stepped up to the front and read from the Bible. "For all have sinned, and come short of the glory of God." She turned a few pages and read another passage. "For the wages of sin is death; but the gift of God is eternal life through Jesus Christ our Lord." After the reading she continued to talk about the verses, explaining their meaning and message to those who had come to hear. When she finished her lesson, she invited anyone who wanted prayer to stay after the service and pray with the missionaries. Art and Gladys Reifel, a young couple in their twenties, stepped forward and stood beside Miss Hollenbeck. They had come to Salka six years earlier and lived in the mission compound just outside the village.

Jacob felt the pull of God on his heart and wanted to go pray with the white people, but fearing the consequences that would come upon him if his father found out, Jacob decided he should leave. As he walked from the building, he felt no joy and happiness. Sin lingered like a heavy weight in his heart, and Jacob knew he needed to do something about his spiritual condition.

That night Jacob tossed and turned, unable to sleep as he worried about the state of his soul. As he pondered the situation, God again impressed upon Jacob that he needed to repent of his sins and accept the salvation offered to him. He rose early the next morning and went to Indazo's home.

When he found his friend, Jacob said, "What you shared with me is real. I want to become a Christian today. Not tomorrow. Today. Right now if possible."

Indazo smiled and replied, "I thank God because He has made Himself known to you. Let us go to the bature's house."

Indazo led Jacob to the home of the Reifels, but before they entered the white people's home, Indazo paused. "You have never been around the white people, have you?"

"Not much."

"Don't be afraid of them," Indazo instructed. "They are people just like us."

"Okay, fine," Jacob replied, still feeling an urgency inside. He needed God and was willing to talk to a person of any color if it would relieve the pressure in his heart.

They entered the Reifels' home, and after brief introductions, Jacob told the missionary, "I want to follow the Lord Jesus Christ."

The tall, dark-haired missionary threw his arms around Jacob and shed tears of joy. During the Reifels' six years in Salka, the Kambari had been very resistant to the gospel. Whenever a villager accepted the Lord, the missionaries felt a great sense of triumph and joy. The group sat down in the living room and the missionaries prayed with Jacob in his language.

After they concluded their prayers, they told him, "Now, you should personally ask Jesus to be your Savior."

Jacob bowed his head and asked Jesus to come into his heart.

As soon as Jacob finished praying, he felt a great change inside! God had worked a transformation in his heart, and he found peace and joy he had never before experienced. "I feel like a new person on the inside," he told his friends, his eyes wide with wonder.

Jacob felt incredibly thankful for these missionaries who left the comfort of their homes in a distant land and came to live among the Kambari. Only through their sacrifice could someone like Jacob learn about the Lord Jesus Christ.

• • •

Though Jacob was excited about his conversion to Christianity and the changes taking place in his heart and life, he realized his father would view the decision to follow a new religion as an act of disobedience. Jacob went to his aunt Apalu and shared the news of his conversion, partly because he wanted to share the remarkable experience with this woman who loved him, and partly because he thought Apalu might intervene on Jacob's behalf if his father became angry when he discovered the news.

Apalu was not happy to hear Jacob's confession. "You have abandoned our forefathers' gods," she accused. "The gods will be angry, and you will be cursed."

When Jacob refused to renounce his Christian beliefs, she grudgingly accepted the change. "There is nothing I can do. Even though I don't approve, I can't stop you, Jacob."

Soon, one of the villagers told Bagudu that Jacob had been seen at the Christian church services and had accepted the white man's God as his own. As Jacob and his father walked to the field, preparing to tend the crops together as they did each day, Bagudu questioned Jacob about the rumors.

"The people are saying you have been to the white man's church. Is this true?"

"Yes," Jacob answered. He had known he could not keep his conversion a secret for long. Now he would face the consequences.

"Are you following the white man's religion?" his father asked, eyes narrowed in anger.

"Yes, Father, I am a Christian, but I have discovered it is not just a white man's religion."

"You have disobeyed me, Jacob! And you know if a man turns his back on the fetish, the gods will curse him and he will die. I fear for your life."

"Father, if you will just listen—" As Jacob tried to explain, he dared to look his father in the eye.

The Kambari considered looking an authority figure in the eye to be an act of defiance or insolence, and Jacob's father grew angry. "Why are you talking to me like that?"

Jacob tried to pacify his father, but to no avail.

"You will not continue your Christian faith! You will return to the fetish," Bagudu raged.

When Jacob refused, Bagudu grabbed a stick and began to beat his son. Jacob turned and fled. He knew many other Christians had suffered similar persecution from their families, so he was not surprised by his father's reaction. He was only sad that his father did not understand his new faith or appreciate the joy he had found in Christ.

Later, his father spoke to him about the situation again. "If you continue serving the white man's God, you will have to leave my house."

Fearing for his safety, Jacob packed a few possessions and went to Indazo's home, hoping to find refuge there. But Indazo's father was not a believer. He, too, disapproved of the boys' conversions. When he discovered Bagudu was angry, Indazo's father grew fearful. He could not afford to incur the anger of the chiefmaker's family. So Indazo's father met with Bagudu to discuss the situation.

When the men sat down to talk, Bagudu made his displeasure known. "Your son led mine into the Christian faith. He was the cause of all this," he told Indazo's father. "I am going to lose my son because of it."

After the talk, Indazo's father refused to allow Jacob to stay in his home and ordered both boys to leave.

Not sure what to do or where to go, the boys turned to the missionaries for help. Art and Gladys Reifel had returned to the United States on furlough, leaving Isabelle Hollenbeck in charge of the mission station. When she heard the boys' stories, she offered to let them live and work on the mission grounds. The boys shared a small hut and helped with the garden and other chores to earn their keep.

While Jacob was thankful for the place to live and the work to keep him busy, his dream of becoming a teacher still burned in his heart. As the weeks passed, he prayed for an opportunity to continue his schooling.

After a time, Jacob approached Miss Hollenbeck with an idea. "I heard there was a mission school in Zuru."

"There is an excellent school there," she replied. "Are you interested in continuing your education?"

"Yes," Jacob assured her. "Indazo and I want to go there."

Miss Hollenbeck approved of the idea. The boys would receive an education and solid Christian training in Zuru. During the next few weeks, she wrote letters and made arrangements for the boys to attend the missionary-run school. Early one December morning, she prayed a blessing over the two young men and said goodbye as they started their long walk to Zuru.

5

Chapter Five

Lead On, O King Eternal

After three days walking the hot, dusty road, Jacob and Indazo trudged into Zuru, weary of traveling and eager to find the school. After asking directions, they arrived at the United Missionary Society (U.M.S.) School and located Rev. Paul Ummel and his wife, Phoebe, the school's managers. Rev. Ummel was a studious-looking man with dark eyes and glasses. Mrs. Ummel wore her long hair pulled back in a bun, accenting her bright smile. The couple greeted the boys with warm smiles and hugs. "Jacob, Indazo, we've been expecting you. Welcome to U.M.S. Zuru."

Jacob smiled at his new principal. "It's good to be here."

Rev. Ummel placed a hand on each boy's shoulder and guided them toward a large building to one side of the campus. "I imagine you boys are tired. Why don't I show you to your rooms in the dormitory. Later, someone will give you a tour of our facilities."

Jacob and Indazo gratefully followed him to their rooms in the dormitory where they would live for the next few years. The boarding school accommodated around four hundred students, many of whom were from the Dakkarkari tribe, which inhabited that area of Nigeria. Like Jacob and Indazo, children from other tribes also had found their way to the school, so the boys were not the only newcomers. Because the Nigerian school year follows the calendar year, many new students were arriving for the

January term.

"Take some time to settle in," Rev. Ummel told them when he had showed them to their rooms. "Tomorrow we will talk about your tuition."

The school requested nominal fees from its students to help cover the expenses of food and shelter. Though the amount was small, some students and their families experienced difficulty paying the tuition, lacking financial resources for various reasons. Estranged from his family, Jacob did not have financial support to pay for an education at a Christian school.

The next day, the boys sat with Rev. Ummel in his office and listened as he explained the school's policies regarding tuition. "While the Missionary Church covers most of our expenses, we do require a small tuition to help buy food and supplies for the children under our care."

Jacob stirred in his chair, fearful that his lack of money would ruin his chance at an education. But Rev. Ummel had a plan.

"Miss Hollenbeck explained your special circumstances to us, and we have a solution. The teachers and missionaries here on the school compound work hard and keep long hours. A few of them would like to hire someone to do chores around their homes an hour or two each day. Would you boys be willing to participate in this work exchange program? Your help will alleviate the workload for our missionaries, and the pay would cover the cost of your tuition."

Joy surged through Jacob. Once again, God had provided for his needs. "We would be honored to assist the missionaries in their homes."

"Jacob, I am assigning you to Miss Luella Landry. She is getting on in years and needs a strong, capable person to help her with her garden and housework."

Jacob smiled. "Yes, sir. I will help Miss Landry in any way I can."

Rev. Ummel turned to Indazo. "My wife and I could use your help in our home."

Indazo nodded. "Thank you, sir."

"Excellent." Rev. Ummel looked pleased to have made an arrangement that benefited all the parties involved. "After school, stop by the house you've been assigned and ask what needs to be done."

When Jacob reported for work his first day, he saw how much Luella Landry needed assistance. Gray-haired, stooped shoulders and hands curling with arthritis, she was unable to perform any heavy lifting, and her arthritis prevented her from doing tasks that required manual dexterity.

"Miss Landry, what can I do to help you?" he asked.

She offered him a grateful smile. "Come sit with me, and we will make a list."

• • •

Just three months into the school year, Indazo's father arrived in Zuru and sought out his son at the school. "I want you to come home and help me on my farm. I am making good money on the ground nuts, but I need someone who can read and write to deal with the buyers."

"I don't know," Indazo replied, reluctant to leave the school and Jacob.

"If you come back home and help me, I will buy you a brand new bicycle." Indazo's father knew just how to tempt him. A bicycle was a coveted prize for a Kambari boy, and Indazo could not resist.

"I suppose I could attend the night classes the Reifel's teach. That way I can continue my education and help you on the farm." So Indazo bid Jacob goodbye and returned home with his father in time to help with the spring planting. While Jacob was glad Indazo and his father had reconciled, he felt the aching loneliness of losing his closest friend.

Yet, while he was saying goodbye to one friend, Jacob was gaining many others. The students at U.M.S. offered good companionship, and Jacob's easy smile and amiable personality made him well-liked among his peers. Jacob developed friendships with several young people, including a lovely young girl named Rose Magani from the Dakkarkari tribe. Rose possessed a keen intelligence and did well in her studies, an important quality to Jacob who valued education. Perhaps a more important and attractive quality, Rose had a close relationship with God and demonstrated a Christian maturity that Jacob admired. Jacob enjoyed spending time in her company and the two passed many an afternoon together.

• • •

Jacob hurried to Miss Landry's home after school, eager to do his chores and return to the dorm to study. She met him at the door, clutching her hands and wearing a pinched look on her face.

"Are you all right, Miss Landry?" he asked.

"It's my hands, Jacob. They hurt so much today." During the months Jacob had worked for the elderly woman, the pain in her hands had worsened until it became crippling at times, turning her hands to claws and bringing tears to her eyes.

"Can I do something to ease your pain?"

She shook her head. "If you will see to the garden, I will be fine. I need to do some dishes, then I will rest."

Jacob harvested some lima beans and ground nuts from the garden, brought them to the front porch and was spreading them out to dry when he heard a loud crash inside the house. Concerned for Miss Landry, he rushed inside and found her standing near the sink in tears. Broken shards of a plate lay scattered across the floor.

"Are you all right, Mallama?"

Her eyes brimmed with tears. "My hands, Jacob. The muscles are cramping and it hurts so badly I can hardly bear it." She held out her hands and Jacob could see the cramping had twisted them into gnarled claws. "Help me," she pleaded.

He rushed to her side and led her to a chair. "How?"

"Press my hands out flat. It's the only way to alleviate the cramps."

Jacob took her thin, wrinkled hand between his and slowly uncurled her fingers, working against the effects of arthritis and age until the cramping passed. "Thank you," she whispered when she finally felt relief from the pain. "I'm afraid my days here are coming to an end, Jacob. In my mind and heart, I am a missionary, but my body reminds me daily that I am also an old woman. I think I will have to retire soon."

In September, a new teacher named Naomi Everett arrived. The children found Miss Everett beautiful, with her dark hair, blue eyes, and willowy frame. The students quickly fell in love with their new teacher, and worked hard to please her. After a short time of training, Miss Everett assumed Miss Landry's teaching position so the older woman could return to the United States and retire. The twenty-four-year-old Miss Everett proved friendly, hard-working and kind, which won her the children's admiration. They gave her a Nigerian name, Mallama Kande. Mallama means "teacher," and Kande means "daughter following the birth of two sons." She did not bother to tell them the name incorrectly described her birth order because she liked the sound of it.

Shortly after Miss Landry left Nigeria, Miss Everett approached Jacob about his assistance. "Jacob, I understand you were a great help to Miss Landry, and I wondered if you would consider working for me now that she is gone."

Jacob, who had worried about his tuition fees since discovering that

Miss Landry was leaving, quickly agreed to Miss Everett's offer. So Naomi Everett assumed Jacob's sponsorship, enabling him to remain in her classroom. In return, Jacob visited her house each day to perform basic chores. Usually he came after doing his homework, but on occasion he came early before school. Naomi greatly appreciated the help. While younger and stronger than Miss Landry, she needed help just as much. As a missionary and teacher, she kept a very busy schedule. Jacob assisted her with chores she could not do herself or did not have time to do after her long workdays.

To reduce expenses, most missionaries kept a garden. With his farming experience, Jacob had no trouble tending the plants and harvesting the crops. Before the rains began in late March, he trekked out into the bush and gathered some long bamboo poles. He brought these back and staked the plants. If left unsupported, the plants would drape across the wet ground and rot. Jacob was responsible for harvesting the ground nuts and spreading them on the veranda to dry. He gathered the lima beans, shelled, peeled, and dried them. Miss Everett sometimes sent Jacob to buy onions from the camel drivers when they came down from the sub-Sahara. These also had to be spread on the veranda and dried somewhat so they would not spoil. What they did not eat immediately was stored in a little, round, mud hut behind Miss Everett's home, but storing food presented some problems. Rats found the food stores an irresistible temptation and regularly invaded the hut.

"Jacob, the rats raided the storage hut again last night. If we can't figure a way to keep them out of my food, I'm not going to have anything to eat." Jacob and Miss Everett barred the door, but the rats only climbed the walls and burrowed through the grass roof. They hung food from ropes or wires, but the rats just shimmied down and gorged on the food while dangling at the end of the line. Keeping the rodents out of the food seemed impossible.

"Don't worry, Mallama. I will find a way to keep the rats away from your food." Determined to solve this problem for Miss Everett, Jacob took stock of his supplies and began to build. Using wire, bamboo and sheets of wire mesh he constructed a barrier to keep the rats away. Jacob hung wire from the grass roof and suspended several layers of wire mesh from the ceiling. He placed the onions and other foods between layers of wire mesh, effectively foiling the rats' raids.

In the house, Jacob was assigned the task of draping the mosquito nets over the beds in the evening. He also rolled the grass mats hanging from the veranda roof up or down, depending on whether Miss Everett wanted sun or shade.

In addition to the physical chores, Jacob also helped and encouraged Miss Everett as she learned to speak Hausa, a necessary skill in her classroom. "How do you say this in Hausa?" Miss Everett asked, pointing at a word or sentence on her paper.

Jacob studied the line and wrote a Hausa equivalent for her, then patiently recited the words until she had learned the proper inflections and pronunciations.

Teachers at the missionary school taught classes of about forty children and often faced tremendous language barriers. The children came from many different tribes, each with its own tongue or dialect. English was taught at the school, but this was a difficult subject to learn. To facilitate classroom studies, some of the early classes were taught in Hausa, the trade language used among the tribes. But often students did not even know this language. Teachers simply had to be clever and creative, doing what they could to teach despite the challenges in communicating. Since Miss Everett was just learning Hausa herself, her task was doubly hard.

In the classroom, Jacob proved to be a very bright student. The children, all Nigerian, took great pride in their class rankings and worked hard to make good scores. Each term Jacob and one other boy competed for first place in classroom standings. While they both made high scores on their work, Miss Everett saw a big difference in the boys' skills.

She said, "When exam time came, this other student would have all the information in his answers, but he had just reproduced my notes word for word on his paper. This didn't really tell me that he had learned or necessarily understood anything. It just told me he was very good at memorizing. Jacob, however, had the answers in his own words, and I knew that he had both understood and learned. I often said that Jacob would go much further than this other student, and years certainly have proven that to be right."

In addition to being a good student, Jacob brought a gift of laughter and joy to the classroom. Miss Everett wrote a word on the chalkboard then turned to her class. "Who can tell me what this word means?"

She scanned the room, waiting for a volunteer. Her gaze fell on Jacob, who in turn made a silly face at her. His antics caught her by surprise, and a giggle escaped her lips. "Jacob, what are you doing?"

The children found her loss of composure humorous and began to laugh. Miss Everett appreciated Jacob's sense of humor and loved him for making her classroom a joyous place, full of smiles and laughter.

• • •

Miss Everett appreciated Jacob's initiative, both in the classroom and in her home. "Some of my favorite people are those to whom I could give some kind of assignment and then forget about it, because I knew it would be taken care of. Jacob was one of those persons who didn't always need everything carefully detailed and outlined for him. He could think it through and follow through himself."

Oftentimes, when Miss Everett was particularly busy, she would ask Jacob to fix her something for dinner. The refrigerator usually held some leftovers, so Jacob only had to warm the food and have it ready to serve. Although the task sounded easy, it was not as simple as one might think. From a Nigerian perspective, the white people had some pretty strange ways. For one, they kept house much differently than the Nigerians. The missionaries set the table, washed dishes and cooked food in a manner that seemed strange to the nationals. The foods they prepared and ate were very different from the Nigerian menu, so Jacob had no experience cooking western food. But being a good steward, Jacob was willing to accommodate Miss Everett to the best of his ability.

One night as he attempted to prepare a meal for dinner, Jacob decided to make soup. He searched the refrigerator, looking for ingredients he could use in his efforts. He found some leftover bread dressing and to his eyes, it appeared to be an excellent soup ingredient. So he made Miss Everett some dinner—dressing soup.

After work, she arrived home, hungry and ready for a meal. Jacob served a bowl of his creation. As soon as the first bite passed her lips, her eyes widened and her lips puckered. Wondering what ingredients he had used to make the soup, she asked, "Jacob, what did you put in here?"

He showed her the container of dressing, and she began to laugh. Realizing his mistake, Jacob joined her, laughing at his own error. They poured the soup down the drain, and Miss Everett helped Jacob prepare something edible.

• • •

Jacob enjoyed the comradery among the students at the Christian school. Unlike his government school experience, the children at U.M.S. acted more like brothers and sisters than classmates. The sense of family helped many students stave off the pangs of homesickness often experienced at boarding schools.

While earning his education, Jacob also received his first taste of leadership. The teachers met to discuss which students might be eligible to fill the role of school prefect—a student leadership role in the private school.

"We have several students with exceptional grades," one teacher noted.

"Yes, but we also need someone who has demonstrated responsibility. He or she will oversee many tasks at the school."

"And don't forget honesty and integrity," another teacher added. "We need someone we can trust in this position."

The teachers and administrators discussed the students on the list and in the end decided Jacob was the best candidate. Now age sixteen, he was proving to be an exceptional student, and his character was evident to his teachers. Jacob won the appointment and readily accepted his new responsibilities.

As prefect, Jacob assigned the students to perform tasks and chores to help clean and maintain the school facilities. Blackboards needed to be cleaned and washed, classroom floors swept before morning classes began. He ensured the dorm rooms were kept clean, enforced curfew and made sure kids were up and ready for classes in the mornings. The children also helped in the garden and performed small errands when necessary. Jacob assigned tasks and made sure the children followed through with their responsibilities.

The position offered Jacob many opportunities and experiences to increase his leadership abilities. He learned to delegate responsibilities, motivate people, and deal with problems in a diplomatic manner—all skills he would use later in life.

Learning came easily to Jacob. His prior years of schooling combined with his keen intellect put him at the head of the class, and his outgoing personality made him an entertaining speaker. His teachers and school administrators saw his skills and asked Jacob to serve as substitute teacher when, on occasion, a teacher could not teach his or her class.

Rev. Ummel or another member of the administration would call Jacob to the offices. "Jacob, one of the teachers is feeling ill and needs to see a doctor tomorrow. Would you be willing to take her classes?"

"I would be happy to do that, sir."

"Thank you, Jacob. We appreciate your willingness to help. Here are the texts used in that classroom. Let me know if you need anything else."

Jacob took a stack of books home, read the texts the teacher indicated and prepared a lesson to present to his peers. Because Jacob had demonstrated academic excellence in the classroom and good leadership as prefect, he earned the admiration of the other children. So when he stood before them as their instructor, they respected his authority. The responsibility gave him his first taste of teaching in a formal setting, an experience that increased his desire to become an educator.

• • •

In Kambari tradition, a boy's parents arrange his marriage for him. While he is still very young, maybe six or seven years of age, his parents choose a girl from the tribe whom they feel will make their son a good match when the children are grown. Parents of the son secure the arrangements with a gift to the girl's parents.

Due to the circumstances surrounding his birth, Jacob's family had not arranged a marriage during his pre-adolescent years. They realized the oversight when Jacob was a teen, attending school at Zuru. Without his knowledge his family decided to correct the problem.

While on a break from his studies at U.M.S., Jacob returned to Salka to visit family and friends. One of his close friends came to warn him of the plans being made behind his back.

"Jacob, your family has arranged a marriage for you. They have been waiting for you to return home and plan to force you to marry now that you are here."

"But I do not want to marry now. Nor do I want to marry a pagan." Since his conversion to Christianity, Jacob had grown in his faith and realized the importance of marrying a strong Christian woman. He wanted a spouse who would share his faith and his ministry, not just his home.

While his desire to marry a Christian woman was strong, his options were few. The Kambari tribe was very gender-lopsided when it came to Christianity. Kambari women were not allowed to participate in Magiro worship, and were taught that religion was a husband's responsibility. For centuries, the women had been encouraged to leave religious matters to the men.

While the Christian religion allowed and encouraged female participation, years of tradition were difficult to overcome. A handful of Kambari men and boys had adopted Christian beliefs, but the women showed little interest. Very few women had converted, leaving Jacob no good candidates for a wife. He knew if his family forced him to marry, he would be wed to a pagan.

His friend shrugged. "You know the ways of the tribe. It is the family's right to arrange your marriage. If you stay, you will have to obey."

"Then I will not stay." Before his family could ambush him, he sneaked out of town and returned to the school in Zuru. Realizing Jacob did not intend to cooperate, his family eventually dropped the matter.

• • •

"Jacob, I have a surprise for you," Miss Everett told him one day. "Come to my house Sunday evening, and I will show you."

Eager to know what treat Miss Everett had in store for him, he hurried to her house late Sunday afternoon.

"Look here," she said, leading him toward a windowsill in the front room. "I've purchased a radio." At that time, very few radios could be found in Zuru, but Miss Everett had managed to obtain one.

"I thought you might like to listen to E.L.W.A. with me this evening. There's a man preaching tonight who I think will interest you."

Radio Station E.L.W.A. (Evangelizing Liberia West Africa) broadcasted messages from several preachers, including Billy Graham and Howard O. Jones. Jacob sat transfixed as the messages of hope and life spilled from the little radio.

When the programs were ended, Miss Everett switched off the radio and talked with Jacob. "Jacob, would it surprise you to know that Rev. Jones is a black man?"

"Really?"

"Yes, he is an African-American. I know you have not seen any with your own eyes, but there are many African men who love the Lord and preach the gospel."

Wanting to hear more of Rev. Jones's messages, Jacob asked his teacher if he could come to her house each Sunday night to listen to the preaching on E.L.W.A. Miss Everett encouraged his interest, of course, and granted him permission. Nearly every Sunday, Jacob came to Miss Everett's living room to listen to the radio broadcast. Hearing an African man preach issued a challenge to Jacob's heart. Because the missionaries had been spreading the gospel message in Nigeria only a short time, there were very few African pastors. Although Jacob was a fairly new Christian, he was feeling God tug at his own heart, urging him toward a life of ministry and preaching.

On one particular Sunday evening, Naomi Everett was not at home when Jacob came to listen to the radio. Because he frequently worked around the house unattended, he had permission to go inside even when no one was present. He let himself in, turned on the radio, and began to listen to his favorite program. When other people were present during the broadcast, Jacob would sit very still, careful to be polite and quiet. But on this particular day, no one was around to observe his behavior.

Abandoning his inhibitions, Jacob gave into an urge that had plagued him for weeks. He stood before the mirror. While Rev. Jones preached, Jacob gestured dramatically and moved his mouth, pretending to be a preacher like Rev. Jones. As the minutes passed, he grew more dramatic, studying his reflection as he mimicked a preacher's actions.

"Jacob, what are you doing?" Naomi asked, laughing.

Jacob whirled around and found his teacher in the doorway staring at him with amusement written on her pretty features. She had returned home sooner than expected and caught him in the middle of his preaching practice. He felt embarrassed that his teacher saw him being so dramatic, and they both had a good laugh. But while he and his teacher laughed about the incident, Jacob knew God was speaking to his heart, calling him to teach and preach the gospel.

* * *

After three years, Jacob graduated from the missionary school program. With several government dignitaries in attendance, Jacob received honors as the top-ranking student in his class. After the presentation of diplomas the children sang a hymn in English—"Lead on O King Eternal," by Earnest W. Shurtleff, 1888.

Lead on, O King eternal,
The day of march has come;
Henceforth in fields of conquest
Thy tents shall be our home.

Through days of preparation
Thy grace has made us strong;
And now, O King eternal,
We lift our battle song.

During her years as teacher, Miss Everett had impressed upon the children that no matter where they went or what they did in life, they would succeed if they listened to God's voice and allowed Him to lead. She taught them the hymn in the hopes that they would carry the message with them wherever they went. Jacob never forgot the song or her admonitions, and in years to come he often sang it to himself as a reminder to listen for God's call and follow His voice.

• • •

After Jacob's graduation, the Missionary organization's district board asked to meet with him.

"Jacob, we're very impressed with your performance in the school as student and prefect. As a result, we would like to make you an offer. We want to start a primary school in Salka and wondered if you would consider serving as the school's headmaster."

Up to that point, the missionaries in Salka had offered an evening class in an effort to improve literacy among the tribe's children. As the sun set in the evening, families came in from the fields. The missionaries would ring the school bell, calling the young men and boys to the classroom.

The boys spent an hour at the church in town learning to read and write the Hausa language while their parents returned home to prepare dinner. Primers and other teaching materials were often in short supply, but the missionaries had Hausa Bibles. While learning to read, the children also learned about God and his ways, so the classes served a twofold purpose.

The desire and need for education among the Kambari had increased beyond the simple training provided in those short evening classes. The Christians especially wanted their children to learn to read and write so they could study the Bible. Parents could send their children to Zuru, but the school was very far away, and the roads between the two towns had proved hazardous. More than once, a truck carrying children to Zuru had crashed. In addition, parents wanted to keep their children close to home. The people asked the missionaries if a school could be started in Salka. They were willing to pay tuition to help fund the effort.

Jacob listened to the board's explanation and asked a few questions about the job description. Enthusiasm bubbled up inside him as he recognized the hand of God at work in his life. Through his service as prefect and substitute teacher in Zuru, God had already provided Jacob with the training he needed to fill this position. "I would be honored to accept the position. It will provide me an opportunity to serve my people and teach the Kambari children, a fulfillment of the dream I've carried in my heart for many years."

Several weeks later, he moved into a hut on the mission compound near the school. Jacob's tribesmen welcomed him back to Salka. He was the first person from the village to graduate with a formal education, and he had graduated at the head of his class, as well. The community took pride in twenty-year-old Jacob's accomplishments, and he was treated as something of a celebrity in Salka, a significant change from his previous status.

Despite the treatment he'd received as a youth, Jacob did not hold a grudge against his tribesmen. Looking back, he could see God's plan in the events surrounding his birth. God had taken a bad situation and used it to bring good into Jacob's life.

Shortly after Jacob's arrival in Salka, Bagudu came to visit him. "I am glad you are back, Son." The two had barely interacted since Jacob's conversion and the subsequent argument with his father.

Jacob embraced the opportunity to reconcile and make peace. "I am glad to be back, Sir. How is the farm?"

His father shrugged. "It could be better. I am only one man, and working by myself I cannot do much."

"Why don't you hire some hands to help you?" Jacob asked, noticing how tired his father looked.

"I cannot afford the expense."

Jacob felt a surge of compassion for the man. Superstition had separated them and deprived Bagudu of his only living son. If circumstances had been different, Jacob would have grown up working in the fields alongside his father, helping to provide for his family. He sensed God was presenting him with an opportunity to reclaim some of the lost years.

"Father, I cannot come and work in your fields because I have a job to do here at the school. But I can give you a portion of my paycheck to hire men to work in my place."

At first Bagudu balked. "No, I could not accept your money."

Jacob insisted and finally his father agreed.

"This school you have started, it is a good thing for our people."

Though the two did not discuss the subject openly, Jacob sensed that his father had accepted his conversion to Christianity and was proud of his accomplishments in his educational pursuits. From that day onward, they enjoyed an amicable relationship.

• • •

As headmaster and teacher at the primary school, Jacob had many opportunities to draw on the experiences and training he had received in Zuru. Because he had organized many school functions and activities during his student years, he was well equipped to handle the running of a boarding school and the one hundred twenty children in his care.

Because parents were not present to oversee their children at the boarding school, Jacob ensured that children were clean and cared for physically—a task which sometimes challenged him.

"Young man, your hair is growing long. Do you think you should visit the mawanzami (barber)?" Jacob had noticed the child's unkept appearance and finally found a private moment to speak with him.

"I asked my parents to send money for a haircut, but they can't afford it. There is nothing I can do about it."

Jacob realized that if he wanted the children to have a well-groomed appearance, he would have to take personal responsibility for their care. "Come to my hut tonight and we will see about your hair, young man."

The boy arrived at the hut later that day, and Jacob led him to a chair.

"What are you doing, Sir?" the child asked, looking uncertain.

"I am going to cut your hair."

The child looked skeptical, but he cooperated. That first haircut did not look quite as good as the barber's work, but Jacob had many opportunities to improve his skill. During his time as headmaster he gave many haircuts, ordered children to bathe, mended and washed clothes, and provided other guidance and assistance normally given by a parent.

Serving as headmaster, teacher, and surrogate parent kept him busy, but he also found time to volunteer at the church in Salka. He taught a Sunday School class every week and led worship when on occasion the usual leader was not able. His life in Salka brought him tremendous satisfaction and joy, for which he thanked God.

6

Chapter Six

Rose

After graduation, Jacob moved to Salka while Rose Magani returned home to her family. Despite the distance between them, the two stayed in contact. They had grown close during their school years, and now that Jacob had finished with his schooling and had a steady job, he wanted to make her his wife.

They wrote letters, and during school breaks, Jacob visited her.

"Indazo, may I borrow your bike?"

"Where are you going?" Indazo asked. He valued the bike his father had purchased for him and kept careful track of it.

"I want to ride to Yelwa this weekend."

Indazo studied Jacob's face carefully. "What's in Yelwa?"

Jacob could not hide his smile. "Rose."

"She must be special if you are willing to ride nearly forty miles to see her."

Jacob pretended not to notice Indazo's curiosity. "May I borrow the bike?"

Indazo nodded. "Just bring it back in good shape."

Jacob's visits usually consisted of a few hours sitting with Rose and her siblings in the Magani house. Sometimes Jacob and Rose went for walks, chaperoned by one of Rose's sisters or brothers. Their friendship deepened, and Jacob suspected she was the woman God intended him to marry. He decided to speak to her about his feelings.

"Rose," he said on one occasion when they had a moment of privacy. "I think you know that I care for you. Would you consider marrying me if I were to ask?"

Rose smiled. "I am agreeable to the idea if my parents give their permission."

Jacob's heart swelled with joy. She returned his affections, as he had suspected. Before he could officially ask Rose to marry him, he had to speak with her parents. They were early Christian converts of the Dakkarkari tribe and now served as pastors at the mission station in Yelwa.

The thought of facing Rose's father with such a monumental request intimidated Jacob. Pastor Magani usually wore a serious expression, and he was a very tall man, in contrast to Jacob who was only five feet, six inches. In addition, tribal cultures within Nigeria are very distinct. The people value their heritage and normally marry someone within their own tribe in order to preserve their customs and culture. In the Dakkarkari tradition, a man must work for his bride-to-be's father for seven years before the two young people are free to wed. Jacob had not fulfilled this obligation.

As a Christian Jacob felt free to marry whomever he chose, but a Kambari man asking to marry a Dakkarkari woman was extremely unusual. He suspected some of the family members would object to Rose marrying an outsider. He only hoped their objections would not sway Pastor Magani's choice against the union.

Because of all the obstacles, Jacob did not know how to approach Rose's father to ask for her hand. After much nervous deliberation, he decided to write a letter. He put the request to marry Rose on paper and gave the letter to an older Christian couple he worked closely with in Salka, asking them to deliver it to Pastor Magani. They agreed to serve as his messengers in this important matter and departed for Yelwa.

Some time later, Jacob's friends returned bringing word and a letter. "Pastor Magani said 'Please give us some time to think about it. We want to talk to Rose and pray about your request.'"

Jacob waited anxiously, feeling as if his life hung in the balance. After several anxious weeks, another letter came. "We've prayed about it, and we feel it is the Lord's will that you marry."

The Magani family approved of the union and granted Jacob permission to take Rose as his wife. After receiving the wonderful news, Jacob went to Yelwa more frequently to spend time with Rose and her family and to discuss plans for the wedding.

During these visits, Jacob frequently witnessed Rose crying. In the Nigerian culture of that day, the bride-to-be was expected to show great sadness about leaving her family. Rose, who loved her parents dearly, spent many hours shedding tears. But her distress bewildered the happy groom, who could hardly keep a smile from his face.

"Why do you cry, Rose? Do you not want to marry me?" he asked.

"Of course, I want to marry you, but I love my parents too. I honor them with my tears. I also cry because I am going to leave my family for the first time. I am going to a different town to live among your people. They have different traditions and speak a different language. I do not know if they will accept me, or if I will fit in. I am afraid I will be lonely in your village."

Her words lingered in Jacob's mind. She would be lonely and something of an outsider if she could not communicate with the Kambari. On his next visit, he proposed a solution. "Rose, I think we should learn to speak one another's native languages. I have already learned some Dakkarci while attending school in Zuru and visiting your family here in Yelwa. I would like to learn more of your language until I can speak it fluently. And I could teach you Kambari so you can talk with the people of my tribe when we move to my village after the wedding."

Rose smiled. "I think you have a good idea."

Jacob and Rose gave one another language lessons, and soon they could communicate in either tribe's language.

• • •

A few months before the wedding, a member of Jacob's family came to visit him in Salka. While they were talking, the man mentioned a bit of news that caught Jacob's attention.

"It appears Danladi will be going to an orphanage," he told Jacob. "No one in the family has stepped forward to care for the boy."

Danladi Daudu Dandodo, the son of Jacob's recently deceased cousin, was only two years old. Often when the mother of a young child dies, family members will take responsibility for the child's care. But in this instance, no one felt capable of caring for the two-year-old. At hearing

Danladi would go to an orphanage, Jacob could not help but remember his own precarious beginnings. His aunt's willingness to adopt him had saved his life. Extending his heart to another child seemed a fitting way to express his gratitude.

"I am to be married soon," he told his visitor. "Perhaps Rose and I could adopt the boy."

During his next visit to Rose's village, Jacob explained the situation. "I would like to adopt him. I know it is a lot to ask, getting married and taking responsibility for a child all at once, but I hate to see him go to an orphanage."

Rose listened and considered Jacob's request. "I think we should adopt him," she decided.

Jacob's family agreed to the adoption, and Jacob took the boy into his home. Danladi accompanied Jacob to the primary school each day. When Jacob went to Yelwa for his wedding, Danladi stayed with some relatives, eagerly awaiting the chance to meet his new mother.

• • •

In Nigeria, the groom and his family pay the bulk of wedding expenses. Funding a Nigerian wedding can be a very costly undertaking. Nigerians do not expect to receive a wedding invitation. When they hear that a relative or friend is to marry, they simply come—sometimes in large numbers. Providing food and temporary housing for all these people can create a very large bill.

Jacob's job at Salka provided him with a wage, from which he saved money for the wedding. Thankfully, Rose's parents offered to contribute, and together they were able to host a memorable wedding.

Rose and Jacob met in the mission church in March of 1959 with around seventy-five guests, mostly from the Yelwa church and Rose's family. Rev. Earl Honsberger, a missionary from Canada who was in charge of the Yelwa mission station where Rose's father served as pastor, performed the ceremony. In those days, people did not need to buy an expensive dress or rent tuxedos. The bride and groom simply dressed in attractive Nigerian clothing.

After the ceremony Jacob and his bride went to the Maganis home and shared a meal with some of the missionaries. They spent the night and started for Salka early the next day.

Most of Jacob's friends and family from Salka could not afford to make the long journey to attend the wedding, so when the bride and groom returned to Jacob's hometown, the villagers held a large reception for him. The newlyweds enjoyed much food and celebration with the people of Salka.

Following Kambari custom, the women gathered together all the wedding gifts, carried them into the large central meeting hall, and set them out for display. Rose's parents had purchased suitcases, plates, clothes, and other housewares that the young couple would need. The women set these alongside the gifts from Jacob's friends and family. The newlyweds were blessed to receive all they needed to start a home together.

Jacob's grandfather and other elders of the tribe viewed the gifts and then pronounced a blessing over the new marriage. Afterward, the ladies collected the gifts and carried them to the newlyweds' hut and helped them settle into their new home.

• • •

After serving one year as headmaster, Jacob was disappointed to learn the primary school in Salka was closing.

"I'm sorry, Jacob, but we just can't find the funds to keep the school open," members of the district board told him. "Even with the parents paying a portion of the costs, the expense is more than we can handle right now. We have to close the doors."

Children whose parents could afford to pay for an education were sent to Zuru. The missionaries resumed the hour-long evening classes, teaching the Kambari children who remained in Salka to read and write Hausa. By that time, some of the older children who had completed the program were able to serve as teachers, taking younger children through the paces.

Since the U.M.S. primary school in Salka was closing, Jacob began to search for a new job. He heard the government was in need of agricultural teachers in the public schools across the nation and would train eligible applicants at the Rural Education Center. He applied for a position in the next session and received an invitation to attend the school. The opportunity required Jacob and his new family to move to Minna. So, after a few weeks with family, they loaded their possessions and headed for a new city.

Chapter Seven

Season of Opportunity

As they entered Minna, one of Nigeria's larger cities, Jacob felt a surge of excitement. The program offered at the Rural Education Center would provide him another way to fulfill his teaching aspirations and perhaps help his people. Better yet, the one-year in-service program offered education and hands-on training in addition to a small wage, so he would have a way to support his family and continue his education at the same time.

Jacob and Rose along with their adopted son, Danladi, rented a one-bedroom home near the school and set up house. "We need to find a church," Jacob said several days after they settled in their new home.

Rose nodded. "Our missionaries have not planted a church in Minna yet. We'll have to find a church from a different organization."

Both Jacob and Rose had been converted and educated in Missionary Church programs, so naturally they would seek a Missionary church. With none available they began to examine their options.

"What about this one? Evangel Church of West Africa (E.C.W.A.). They are members of the Sudan Interior Mission organization. I've heard good things about them." Jacob and Rose visited E.C.W.A. and found a church to call home.

Jacob began attending classes at the Rural Education Center Monday through Friday. Once a month, or as the need arose, the class would take field trips to outlying villages to help the farmers and members of the community solve problems and improve their farming capabilities. Jacob, who had worked on family farms since his toddler years, enjoyed learning more about planting crops and raising livestock.

The year of training passed quickly and graduation approached. Jacob expected to be placed in a government school to teach agricultural science, but the school officials had other plans for him. The administrators called him to their offices and made him an offer.

"Jacob, we are in need of another teacher here at our training facility. Because you have made excellent grades and have prior teaching experience, we feel you are the perfect candidate for the job. Would you consider staying here in Minna and training other teachers?"

Jacob discussed the offer with Rose, and she agreed he should take the job. So, he stayed and taught at the school for several years. He was placed in the poultry section of the school, teaching his adult students the finer points of raising chickens and rabbits. The school had incubators for the chicks, which allowed students to raise poultry from hatchlings through the sale. As teachers were sent from the Rural Education Center to impart this practical knowledge in middle school classrooms across the country, their students would graduate with enough knowledge to make a good living at farming or raising livestock, ensuring that no one went hungry.

• • •

While living in Minna, the Bawas added a new member to their family. Grace Talata (Tuesday) Bawa came into the world on a Tuesday, quickly winning her parents' hearts with her tiny smiles and happy coos. A month after her birth, the family moved seventy-eight miles away to Abuja. Jacob's superiors had decided he was ready for promotion, and they transferred him into a supervisory position. He replaced a British officer in overseeing a large area of the country's agricultural projects, assigning tasks to a staff of agricultural officers and also holding training seminars and classes. When he was not teaching, he traveled in a Land Rover to check the progress of agricultural projects and improvements in his district.

While Jacob enjoyed his work with the Rural Education Center, he was not entirely satisfied with the job. He and Rose talked about the subject, and he shared his heart.

"I want to work with children and to teach in a setting that also allows me to minister God's love to my students. At my current job I can't fulfill that call on my life."

"Perhaps you should look for another job. Do you have something else in mind?"

"Yes, but it's not a job." For years he had felt God urging him to attend a Bible college. After counseling with a missionary friend, Jacob felt God leading him to enroll in Ilorin Theological Seminary. Situated in Ilorin, Nigeria, the Missionary Church college taught Bible classes and offered ministerial training to around three hundred students. The teachers and administrators were missionaries from America and Canada.

At the end of the year, Jacob resigned his position with the Rural Education Center and made arrangements to move his family to Ilorin. The agricultural school was reluctant to let a capable employee go, but seeing his determination, they accepted the resignation. Jacob and Rose packed their possessions and prepared to move to a new city. Since they did not own a vehicle of their own, the Bawas arranged to ride one of the lorries (large trucks) that traveled between the cities, hauling trade goods and people.

The week of their departure, heavy rains turned the dirt roads into mud and made traveling difficult. More than once the lorry bogged down in mud, and all the passengers disembarked to help push the vehicle out of the mire. The delays added hours to the journey, extending their travel far into the night. The lorry and its weary passengers arrived in Ilorin at five o'clock in the morning.

As the men unloaded the luggage and freight and distributed it to the passengers, Jacob considered how he would transport his family to the seminary campus. He did not have directions to the school, nor could he call at such an early hour and ask someone to come for them. But his worries about finding his way to the campus were preempted by an announcement from the men unloading the luggage.

"We've unloaded everything, so we will be going now."

Jacob glanced at the pile of luggage clustered around him and Rose and noticed one very important container was missing. "Wait!" he called. "Are you sure you have not overlooked something? I brought a large wooden trunk that has not been returned to me."

The men looked through the truck again and found no container matching Jacob's description. Perhaps it had been left in Minna, or maybe it had tumbled out of the truck somewhere along the road. Maybe a dishonest person had absconded with the box. Regardless of how the trunk had disappeared, it was most certainly gone. "Sorry, it's not here," the men told him. With shrugs and apologetic looks, they boarded the lorry and left.

As Jacob watched them drive away, a sick feeling formed in his stomach and spread throughout his body. The trunk had contained all of Jacob's personal possessions, including a large sum of money for his tuition to the school. All their savings, his clothes, personal items—gone. Without the trunk he had nothing but the clothes on his back, and those were dirty and soiled from pushing the truck.

Disheartened, he gathered his family and their possessions and found his way to the seminary campus. By the time the Bawas arrived, the school principal, Dr. Russell Sloat, was awake to greet them. When Jacob told him what had happened, the man was extremely sorry for the loss. "Don't you worry," he told Jacob. "Everything will work out."

At the time, the Sloats had guests staying in their house, a missionary couple by the name of Brenneman. When Rev. Wayne Brenneman heard about Jacob's troubles, he quickly sifted through his ample wardrobe and donated several pairs of slacks and some shirts. "Go try them on, Jacob," Dr. Sloat urged. They showed him to a bedroom where he could change. Minutes later he emerged laughing. Smaller in stature than the missionary who donated the apparel, Jacob resembled a child playing dress up in his father's clothing. Pant legs dragged on the floor, and shoulder seams dangled midway down his upper arms.

"Not to worry," Mrs. Sloat said, looking him over. "I'm handy with a sewing machine. We'll take them in and hem the pants. They'll fit just fine when I'm finished." Mrs. Sloat set to work, and soon Jacob owned a new wardrobe.

While he had pockets to call his own, he had no money to put in them. "Since my money is gone, I don't think I will be able to attend the school," he told the Sloats.

Despite his lack of funds, the Sloats urged Jacob to stay. "Apply to the school and trust God to supply the tuition, Jacob. I think He has a plan."

Jacob decided to take that advice. Many students worked part-time to pay for their tuition and earn extra spending money. Because Jacob had held jobs during his previous schooling, he knew he could manage.

So Jacob went to the registrar's office to register for classes. "I need to arrange to make payments toward my tuition," he explained to the clerk after he had finished filling out the necessary paperwork.

The person working the desk handed him a receipt and said, "That won't be necessary. Someone has taken care of your fees. You do not owe us any money."

Relief flooded through Jacob, and he praised God for providing the funds he needed to attend the college and prepare for ministry. He later discovered that Miss Isabelle Hollenbeck, who had retired to her home in Brown City, Michigan, was his generous benefactor. While her body had aged and become too weak to endure the rigors of missionary work in Salka, she still desired to contribute to missions. She sent checks to support Jacob's Christian education and cover his expenses.

The school provided the married couple with a dorm room and a small stipend to buy groceries and basic household items. Jacob and Rose also worked part-time at the college to earn money for other needs that arose in their family. As Dr. Sloat had predicted, God provided a way for Jacob to attend Bible college.

. . .

At the time Jacob and Rose transferred to Ilorin, Rose was just months from delivering another child. The couple looked forward to this blessed event; however, they realized the limitations of their circumstances.

"Jacob, you are so busy with classes and responsibilities related to the college, I'm not sure you will be able to give me the help I need when the baby is born."

Jacob understood her concerns. He had been wondering how he would care for Rose, a baby and two toddlers, and meet the demands of college too. "Yes, we probably need to make some plans."

"I've been thinking, maybe I could go stay with my parents in Yelwa for a month. I haven't visited them in ages, and I know my mother would be thrilled to help with Danladi, Grace and the new baby."

They contacted her parents, and Rose received an enthusiastic invitation to bring the children for a visit. One month before her due date, Rose traveled to Yelwa and moved into her parents' home. Grandma and Grandpa Magani lavished affection on their grandchildren and pampered Rose.

One month later, Rose sat listening to the rain pattering against the rooftop when the contractions began. Her parents drove her to the hospital, braving muddy roads and poor visibility to reach the facility. The rain continued all day and night as she labored. Finally, Rose gave birth to a healthy baby boy.

After Rose had returned to her room, her father came to see her and the baby. "I think you should name him Anaruwa (It's raining)," he said. Nigerians often choose a name that corresponds with an event or happening the day the baby is born. Many Nigerians are named after the days of the weeks or weather-related words. But Rose and Jacob had already selected a name: James Bala (Thursday) Bawa.

When the baby was strong enough to travel, Rose's young cousin Salamatu accompanied her back to Ilorin to serve as a live-in babysitter. When the new semester began, Rose also registered for classes. Jacob and Rose attended school Monday through Friday and often did small jobs or had ministry responsibilities in the evening. They appreciated Salamatu, whose faithful care of their little ones allowed them the time they needed to prepare for the ministry they knew God was calling them to perform.

• • •

The Bawas spent three years at Ilorin and forged some wonderful friendships. The students and faculty were very much like family, and the Bawas enjoyed spending time with members of the seminary's community both in and out of the classroom.

The faculty and students came together on Friday evenings to enjoy a time of fellowship. At these gatherings, the students frequently provided entertainment by performing short skits in which they mimicked their professors and school officials. On one occasion, Jacob did an impersonation of Mrs. Witt, the wife of the school's new principal and a teacher at the college.

Jacob strolled onstage wearing a dress and walking as if he wore high heels. Just the sight of him in women's clothing sent the students into gales of laughter. Jacob strutted to center stage, playing his part to the fullest. After his grand and hilarious entrance, he turned toward the audience and, in a high falsetto, delivered a line that Mrs. Witt spoke to her class every morning. "Good morning, everybody. Can we stand for prayer?" The students roared with laughter, and Mrs. Witt found the imitation so funny that she laughed until tears streamed down her face.

• • •

Ilorin's curriculum required students to spend time every Friday afternoon doing personal evangelism. The average Nigerian workday began at 7:30 a.m. and ended at 3:30 in the afternoon. So early Friday evenings, people came home from their jobs and relaxed after a long work week.

Seminary students went into the city of Ilorin to witness door to door or walked through the market, talking to people and sharing the gospel with their city. Some groups piled into a truck and rode to small settlements outside the city. Jacob found this part of his education very rewarding and saw several converts join the church. As a result of the students' efforts, the school's Sunday service was well attended, drawing many of the converts they had affected in their evangelistic endeavors.

Jacob also participated in the college choir, which traveled to different parts of Nigeria. The choir ministered at evangelistic gatherings and also served as a recruiting tool for the seminary. Once a year, the choir went on tour, making stops at all the U.M.S. churches in the circuit. After singing several songs, the choir members took turns sharing their testimonies. They spoke of their salvation experiences and how God had called them to attend Ilorin Theological Seminary in order to prepare them for the ministerial calls on their lives. In sharing testimonies, choir members used their gifts and also drew many new students to the college.

In addition to receiving a wonderful education and experience in ministry, Jacob benefited from the relationships he built with his teachers and school administrators. Grant Sloss, who replaced Russell Sloat as the school principal shortly after Jacob arrived at Ilorin, had a tremendous impact on Jacob's life. Rev. Sloss's Christ-like leadership impressed Jacob. He prayed he would someday be just as effective a leader. Rev. Sloss left the college after Jacob's first year, and Mr. and Mrs. Auburn Witt took over the leadership position.

Around that same time, Isabelle Hollenbeck died, and the Witts assumed responsibility for Jacob's tuition fees so that he could remain at the college. In return, he baby sat their children each evening and performed some simple work. Jacob greatly appreciated the sponsorship and mentoring they provided.

• • •

During the years Jacob studied at Ilorin, Rev. Billy Graham came to Nigeria to hold a crusade. Jacob had admired Billy Graham since listening to his weekly sermons on Naomi Everett's radio at the U.M.S. School in Zuru, and looked forward to attending the crusade. Graham's staff sent inquiries to Christian organizations and institutions in the area, asking for the names of people qualified to translate the sermon from English into the various languages spoken in Nigeria.

Jacob received a phone call. "Billy Graham is in need of bilingual people to translate at the crusade, and your name is high on the list. Would you consider serving as his Hausa translator?" Jacob quickly accepted the invitation, honored to have been chosen.

When the time came, Jacob sat in a little booth with a copy of Graham's message on the desk before him. As Graham spoke, Jacob listened to the message on an earpiece and spoke the translation into a microphone, which relayed the Hausa version to the audience members' headphones. Many of Jacob's friends were in the audience, listening to his translation.

Jacob kept up with the speaker very well until he encountered one word that he could not translate—snow. In the warm Nigerian climate, temperatures never dip low enough to freeze water, so the Hausa language contains no word for snow. At a loss, Jacob sat in silence for a few seconds before deciding to skip that sentence and continue with the rest of the sermon, hoping Billy Graham would not bring up the word snow again.

His friends later teased him about the pause in translation. "Why did you stop speaking in the middle of the sermon?" they asked. "You were talking away and then total silence filled the earset."

Jacob laughed and explained Rev. Graham's use of the word snow. The Nigerians, who had heard of this phenomenon called "snow" but had never seen it, found the incident quite humorous.

• • •

Since the students at Ilorin Theological Seminary were training for ministry, the school required students to take a course on homiletics—the art of preaching. To provide them with opportunities to practice their preaching skills, the college administrators assigned each student a time to minister at the college chapel service, attended by about 1,000 people. Jacob, like all the other students, took a turn at heading chapel. Speaking before his teachers and peers intimidated him, but he made it through his turn and delivered an admirable sermon.

Jacob received word that Mallam Andrawus, the District Superintendent of the Northern Missionary Churches, wanted to meet with him. As Jacob crossed town and made his way to the Missionary

Church Headquarters, located in a different section of Ilorin town, he wondered what had prompted the superintendent to call him. When he arrived at the offices, a secretary led him to one of the guest rooms, where Mallam Andrawus was staying.

The superintendent greeted Jacob with a smile and a handshake. "Good afternoon, Jacob. Thank you for coming."

Jacob took a seat in the chair offered him and waited expectantly to learn why he had been summoned.

"Your excellence in the pulpit, in the classroom, and in your life has earned you the regard of Ilorin's staff. I have a pastorate position open, and when I asked for names of potential candidates, you came highly recommended. The Ilorin police force has formed its own church. The leaders approached the Missionary district board, expressing a desire to become part of the Missionary organization. They also need a pastor, and we would like to offer you the position."

Jacob had to swallow the lump forming in his throat in order to speak. "I am honored you would consider me." The men discussed the responsibilities and expectations related to the job, then Jacob went home to discuss the offer with his wife.   Serving as a pastor would demand a good deal of time, and Jacob wanted to have his wife's blessing and support. After prayer and consideration, Jacob and Rose agreed the offer was God's will for them.

So, in addition to his full-time studies and a part-time job, Jacob went every Sunday and preached at the police church and handled the usual pastoral responsibilities for the 200-member congregation. Although the obligation kept him extremely busy, he gained valuable experience both in preaching and ministering to the spiritual needs of people.

• • •

Throughout his years at Ilorin, God was confirming Jacob's call to preach. But the government continued to approach him. They wrote frequently to offer him positions, hoping to bring him back into government service.

Jacob knew God wanted him to go into ministry. He looked forward to finishing school and pastoring full time. He repeatedly turned down offers from the government, but they refused to give up. Finally, Jacob sent a letter telling them God had called him to preach and teach God's Word, and he intended to devote himself full time to Christian ministry. No government position, no matter how prestigious or lucrative, would entice him away from the path he felt led to follow. Realizing Jacob would not be swayed, they gave up, for the time being, but would later offer him other government positions, which would prove beneficial to both Jacob and the church.

8

Chapter Eight

A Living Example

When Jacob completed his studies at Ilorin in 1963, he met with the district board and its superintendent to receive his ministry assignment. "As you know, Jacob, the Kambari tribe is still largely unresponsive to the gospel. Until now, the missionaries have headed the effort in Salka. While we've seen some success, we wonder if the Kambari would be more receptive to one of their own tribesmen. We would like you to return to your hometown and live as an example before your people. You will serve as pastor in the Salka church and a teacher at the Hausa Bible School with assistance from the missionaries assigned to that station." Jacob accepted the position and became the first Nigerian national to pastor and teach in Salka.

Despite forty years of mission work in Salka, only one hundred of its approximately 2,000 inhabitants had converted to Christianity. The Kambari were slow to accept the gospel, a fact that discouraged the Bawas during their first year there. Jacob loved his people and wanted them to know God's blessings. Two of the people he loved most, his aunt and his father, had not responded to the call even though Jacob had spent years witnessing to them and dedicated his life to the ministry.

Jacob, Rose and their children moved into a parsonage on the mission compound. Shortly afterward, the missionaries held Jacob's ordination ceremony. The school administration had wanted to ordain Jacob in Ilorin, but he requested that the ceremony take place in his hometown so that his father could be there to witness it. During a regional camp meeting in Salka, Rev. Russell Sloat and Mallam Andrawus blessed Jacob and commissioned him to minister in the full capacity of a pastor.

Fulfilling the roles of both pastor and teacher kept Jacob moving from dawn until dusk most days. He taught at the school from early morning until three in the afternoon, then handled his pastoral duties. He led prayer, evangelized, taught baptism classes, visited his congregation in their homes and preached several sermons a week.

Rose also taught Bible courses in the Hausa Bible School, which had become very popular since its inception in 1951. Each year the school sifted through hundreds of applications, narrowing the field to around thirty-five prospective students who showed the most potential. Students came from Missionary churches all across the country and trained to become pastors, Sunday School teachers, Christian leaders and laymen. The Missionary Church's ultimate goal was to equip Nigerian nationals to minister and assume the roles the missionaries had established. The Hausa Bible School was responsible for training many of the nationals to serve as pastors and church leaders in Nigeria's Missionary Church, and Jacob and Rose contributed all they could to the effort.

· · ·

Shortly after moving to Salka, Rose told Jacob they would be having another child. As the months progressed, she continued to work in the ministry, teaching classes and helping wherever she saw a need. Near her due date, Rose and Mrs. Moran (the missionary wife stationed in Salka) taught a class to some of the village women. After class, Rose was gathering her things and preparing to leave when she grew dizzy and fainted. Mrs. Moran and Jacob, who was also nearby, rushed to Rose's aid and helped her back to their home where she could rest.

The following day, Rose went into labor and gave birth to Sarah Lami (Thursday - feminine) Bawa. When the doctors allowed Jacob to visit his wife and daughter, he stared into her crib, amazed at the newborn's size. A much larger newborn than their other children, Jacob understood why his wife had been having difficulty carrying her. The story of the incidents surrounding Sarah's birth became a family favorite, and Jacob liked to say, "It's no wonder that one day before Sarah came into the world, she knocked her mother down."

• • •

When Jacob and his family moved to Salka, Apalu began attending church and faithfully accompanied them each Sunday. She seemed to enjoy the services. She listened to all Jacob and Rose told her about their God. She even admitted a strong interest in Christianity. Yet she had not accepted the Christian faith as her own. Puzzled by her hesitancy, Jacob asked her why she still clung to the fetish worship.

"I respect your beliefs, Jacob. Your religion is good, but I am a leader among the women of the Kambari tribe. I cannot abandon the fetish. It would set a poor example."

For the next few years, Jacob, Rose, and their children continued to witness to Apalu, especially Grace and Sarah, Jacob's girls. Apalu listened intently, but she did not seem concerned enough to make a change.

On one occasion, two-year-old Sarah said to her grandmother, "Kaka, are you happy that we are always together as a family?"

"Yes, I am," Apalu replied. "I am glad you have returned to Salka so I can spend time with you."

Sarah, in her childlike way, appealed to her grandma to accept salvation. "If you would accept Christ as your savior, then someday we will be together forever in heaven."

The child's words struck a chord deep inside Apalu's heart. She loved her family dearly and imagined the happiness she would feel if she could spend eternity with them. Yet, her love for them was not enough to prompt her to convert to Christianity.

A short time later, Apalu grew very ill with a digestive problem. She was confined to her bed for weeks and tried many remedies to cure her illness and relieve the pain in her abdomen. She called upon the pagan gods and drank potions from the medicine man, but her condition worsened.

Finally, Apalu agreed to seek help and healing from the Christian God. Rose and her daughters went to Apalu's hut and laid hands on her, praying that God would bring healing. After a week of daily prayer sessions, Apalu's body began to recover. Because she had tried many remedies and nothing worked until her family came and prayed, Apalu gave God the credit for her healing. When she was well again, she went to the church and accepted Christ, determined to serve the One who had saved her from death. Jacob and his family rejoiced that they had witnessed Apalu's salvation.

Shortly after her conversion, Apalu's second husband died, leaving her widowed. When a Kambari loses a spouse, the tribe believes that evil spirits or curses have targeted the living spouse. No one in the tribe wanted to associate with Apalu for fear they would bring the curse upon themselves. Not concerned with pagan superstitions, Jacob and his family decided to move Apalu into their home and take responsibility for her care.

Around that same time, Rose invited Bagudu to share the evening meal with them each night. His second wife had passed away, and Jacob did not want Bagudu to eat alone in his hut every night. The invitation pleased Bagudu and allowed the Bawas opportunities to witness to him about God's love.

• • •

After working in Salka for a year, Jacob realized that in order to reach the Kambari with the gospel, he and his church would need a targeted evangelistic campaign. To his delight, Dr. Billy Graham announced he was organizing a Congress on World Evangelism. Christian leaders from across the globe were invited to come to Switzerland to discuss evangelism, and Graham's staff asked Jacob to serve as a member of the planning committee. Jacob went to Switzerland one month prior to the event and helped prepare and organize.

Internationally known evangelists spoke to the thousands of ministers who came to the congress. Jacob and his Nigerian counterparts left the conference inspired, determined to implement effective evangelism programs in their cities. Upon returning home, Rev. Swank, another Nigerian and a leader at the conference, developed a national evangelism program called New Life for All. Eager to participate, Jacob attended a training seminar in Jos. When he returned to Salka, he structured the program in his church.

New Life for All required every member of the church to go out and witness once a week. On Sundays, Rose led a group of women to neighboring villages to witness. They strapped their young children to their backs and walked ten miles one way just to share the gospel. The church also held evangelistic meetings in nearby towns. As a result of their efforts, the men and women of many Kambari villages left their fetishes and idol worship and turned to God by the hundreds.

Because many towns lacked a Christian church, Jacob had to help new converts construct a meeting place. He also assigned students and graduates of Hausa Bible School to pastor the many new churches.

After the New Life for All program began to have an impact, the attitude toward Christians changed. Prior to this time, Christians were teased, persecuted and treated very poorly for their beliefs. But as the program swept through the population, the village began to accept the Christians.

• • •

In 1966, the Christians of Salka had much cause for rejoicing when seventeen people from Salka bore witness to their faith in Christ through water baptism. Following a Sunday morning service, a large part of the congregation walked three miles from the town to the scene where a baptismal service would take place. Pastor Jacob Bawa had never baptized anyone before, but after discussing the matter with missionary John Moran, the two agreed it was time for him to do so. John agreed to enter the water with Jacob and baptize the first few candidates while Jacob observed the process. After John performed a few baptisms, Jacob would take responsibility for the rest.

Standing on the shores of the river, Jacob delivered a short message, and each baptismal candidate was encouraged to give a personal testimony. When they had each taken their turn, Jacob and John waded into the water. The mud floor was soft and they sank to their ankles in muck while the water swirled gently around their waists.

As they had agreed, John baptized the first few candidates. After the fifth one, John looked to Jacob. "Are you ready to give it a try?"

"I believe so," Jacob responded.

As the next candidate was led into the water, John watched Jacob's confidence drain away and float downriver. The woman who approached was very tall and quite large. Jacob, who stood about five feet, six inches tall and was of a smaller build, looked almost like a child standing next to the woman. Unwilling to drown his first baptismal candidate, Jacob decided he had better let John do the honors. "Mallam Yahaya (John's name in the Hausa language), she is too big for me!"

John conceded the point and stepped forward to baptize the woman, who endured the whole situation with grace. Pastor Bawa baptized the remaining candidates without incident.

• • •

While Jacob was experiencing ministry adventures with John Moran, their children were creating some mischief. Jacob and John were blessed to have children about the same age who frequently played together, along with the children of the Hausa Bible School students. The children created games to play and could amuse themselves for hours. One afternoon, Jacob's son James and John's son John Jr., along with several Nigerian boys, decided to give James a radical makeover. A pile of ashes from a burned-out trash fire supplied them with the materials they needed for the job.

Soon they presented James to his parents, covered from head to toe with white ashes. When Jacob and Rose saw their son with his skin strangely whitened, they asked, "What have you boys done?"

All smiles, the boys responded, "We have changed James into a bature" (white person).

Like all good ministers, Jacob used stories and illustrations from his life to help teach the gospel. The story of James's attempt to transform himself into a bature later helped Jacob to demonstrate the difference between being changed on the outside—a chore that man can do on his own—and being changed in the heart—a task only God can perform.

• • •

After three-and-a-half years in Salka, Jacob and Rose faced another change in occupation and location. The mission board decided the time had come to prepare Nigerian nationals to assume positions of leadership pertaining to the Missionary Church's ministry in the country. In order to accomplish their goal, the Missionary organization needed to give Nigerians some responsibilities in institutions like Ilorin Theological Seminary. They discussed the matter at their 1966 national conference and decided that Jacob was a prime candidate for promotion.

The board contacted John Moran and asked him to speak with Jacob about the matter. John relayed the information at their next encounter. "Jacob, the Missionary Church would like you to consider going to North America to continue your education."

The request caught Jacob by surprise. "Why do they ask this of me?"

"They are very impressed with your work and service and want to prepare you to assume leadership at Ilorin Theological Seminary. In order to do that, you need to attend a Christian college and obtain a higher degree in Theology than is available to you in Nigeria."

"Who will take over the church here?" Their church had grown to five hundred members, and they had many church plants in other villages. Jacob would not agree to leave unless the church had a capable leader.

"Ezra Dikki is well-trained. If you agree to go, the board will ask him to replace you." Jacob knew Ezra Dikki, a former student at the Hausa Bible School. He had trained under Mrs. Reifel, who headed the Bible School while her husband, Art, traveled through the bush for weeks at a time to minister at distant villages. Ezra would make a fine pastor for the Salka church.

"But what about my family?" Jacob asked. In the performance of his ministry duties, he had traveled away from home for a few weeks at a time and knew his wife and children struggled during his absence.

"You would be living in the dorms and taking a heavy load of classes. Your family would have to stay here in Nigeria."

"I don't know," Jacob said. Several years earlier he would have jumped at the chance, but now he had four children, and Rose was expecting again. How would they manage?

John had developed a deep friendship with Jacob during their years of service together and understood his hesitation. But he also saw the call of God on Jacob's life and encouraged him not to falter in his walk. "Keep in mind, this is only for a season, maybe a year. It won't be easy, but God will sustain you and your family. Talk to Rose about it."

The two men parted, and Jacob returned home to tell Rose about the request. They stayed up long into the night discussing the situation and its implications for their family.

"It would not be practical or financially possible to take the whole family," Jacob pointed out. "We would be separated for a year or more."

Though Rose did not relish the idea of living a continent apart from her husband for a year, she could see the greater purpose. "God is preparing you for His service. You should go."

"What about you and the children?"

"I can stay with my parents for a year. I'm sure they will enjoy having the children nearby, and I can help them in their home and ministry."

When the decision was final and the arrangements made, Jacob and Rose sat down with their young family and told their children. The children responded to the news with tears and protests, especially James who was very attached to his father. Whenever Jacob took short ministry trips, James became so distraught about the separation he made himself sick. Jacob wondered how his son would weather a lengthy separation and regretted leaving Rose to deal with the boy's distress. Gradually, with reassurance from their parents, the children accepted the changes coming to their family.

• • •

Rose was expecting another child as Jacob's departure approached, and the couple prayed she would deliver before he left the country. Just weeks before he was scheduled to leave, Rose felt her time drawing near. "It won't be long now. I think we should drive to the hospital in Tungan Magajiya."

The nearest hospital facilities lay approximately thirty miles north of Salka across dirt roads and bush country. If Jacob wanted Rose to deliver in a hospital, he would need to leave well in advance of her labor. Rose's parents had been transferred from Yelwa to Tungan Magajiya. When her parents heard she was expecting and that she intended to drive to Tungan Magajiya's hospital for the delivery, they offered Jacob's family a place to stay while awaiting the birth.

John Moran drove the couple, and days later Jeremiah Bagudu (named after Jacob's father) Bawa was born. One week after welcoming his newest son whom they nicknamed Jerry into the world, Jacob placed his wife and children in the care of his in-laws. As he said goodbye, he hugged each one and tried to memorize every line of their faces, hoping his memories would sustain him during the long months ahead.

Photographs

*Paul and Mabel Ummel with
Helen and Wesley (1944)*

*Paul and Mabel Ummel with Helen
(1937)*

Isabelle Hollenbeck (1954)

Jacob A. Bawa, Salka, Nigeria
(1957)

Rev. John Bontrager (1967)

Mrs. John (Betty) Bontrager (1967)

Earl Honsberger

Luella Landrey (1954)

Naomi Everett (1958)

Russell and Evelyn Sloat with two of their three children (1954)

Rev. Auburn Witt (1954)

Rev. Russell Sloat (1962)

John and Retha Moran with John Jr. and James (1963)

Dr. Jacob Bawa in classroom at Bethel College (1995-1996)

Rev. John Moran (1963)

Grant and Dorothy Sloss with David and Stephen (1957)

Rev. Grant Sloss (1961)

Hilda, Karen, John and Wayne Brenneman (1956)

Arthur and Gladys Reifel with Eva Mae and Elmer

Rev. Arthur Reifel

Mrs. Arthur (Gladys) Reifel (1976)

Jacob Bawa, second from left; Russell Sloat, far right

(L-R) Emmanuel Akinlowan, Michael Reynolds, Jacob Bawa, Peter Achimugu

Jacob is fourth from right on front row. Missionaries (l-r) Helen & George Schroeder, Harold Knights, Jean Crist, Mary Paulus, Mike Reynolds (visitor from USA), Art Reifel (in back row) and John Bontrager

Jacob Bawa in center; John Bontrager on left

Jacob and Rose Bawa and family

Jacob standing beside an ant hill

Russell and Evelyn Sloat
and their girls

(l-r) Mary Paulus, Betty and
John Bontrager

John Bontrager and
Samuel Oloyede

*John Bontrager and two
UMTC students*

Jacob Bawa (1975)

Jacob Bawa family (1975)

Dr. Jacob and Rose Bawa (1998)

9

Chapter Nine

New Horizons

"As soon as we reach cruising altitude, we will begin serving an in-flight meal."

Jacob heard the captain's announcement and lowered his tray, curious about the food served on an airplane. Thankfully, his missionary friends had introduced him to some of their foods before he left the country. They wanted to help him make the transition into a new and unfamiliar culture.

"Jacob, would you like to have supper with me and a few other mission-aries?" Naomi Everett asked when she stopped by his home one day just weeks before his schedule departure. "We want to give you the opportu-nity to taste Western food and experience Western table manners before you go to North America. You will find their food and customs are very different than your own, and we thought an informal lesson might help you adjust more quickly."

Jacob had wondered about the drastic changes he would face upon moving to another continent. He recognized the wisdom in preparing for the transition. "I'd love to come." A date and time was set for the occasion.

Since Jacob had worked closely with missionaries for years, he had observed the differences in their eating habits and foods. As the dinner drew near, his main concern was not whether he would use the correct utensil but whether the food would fill his rumbling stomach.

As he and Rose discussed plans for the dinner one afternoon, he expressed his concerns. "I have seen the strange-looking foods and small portions the missionaries eat. I doubt the meal will satisfy me."

"You could always eat a little tuwo (guinea corn porridge) before you go. Then if you don't like the food or if they don't serve you enough to fill your stomach, you won't be hungry," Rose suggested.

Her advice made sense to Jacob, and he decided to follow it. The evening of the dinner, Rose prepared tuwo and Jacob ate a hearty bowlful. He arrived at the missionary's home, his stomach already satisfied from his pre-dinner snack. The missionaries escorted him inside and showed him to a seat at the table. Delicious aromas filled the air as his hosts placed dish after dish of enticing food on the table.

When the meal began, Jacob took a small sample of each dish. After a few bites, he realized he'd made a mistake in eating before he came. The food tasted good and was more filling than he had suspected. But because he was nearly full from the tuwo, he couldn't eat as much of the delicious food as he would have liked.

Seeing their guest was not eating much, the missionaries questioned him about the meal. "Don't you like our food, Jacob?"

With a sheepish smile, he confessed to eating before he came. "But I regret eating the tuwo. Your food is very good. I would like to eat more, but my stomach is ready to burst."

The missionaries found his blunder amusing, and the group shared a laugh. Despite his error in judgment, the evening of fellowship and instruction left Jacob feeling better prepared to make the move to North America. Surely the food on the airplane would be similar to the meal his friends had served him.

Soon the stewardess pushed a cart through the aisle beside his row and offered Jacob and the Englishman next to him their meals. As Jacob looked over the contents of the plate, he found several small paper packets. Some were marked: sugar, salt, pepper. One little packet bore no markings or labels to identify it, but he was too shy to ask someone about it.

He glanced at the other passengers, hoping to see someone using the item. No one near Jacob had opened the packet yet. His curiosity grew until he couldn't resist. He tore open the wrapper and pulled out a little white wafer. He had no idea what it was, but white people's food often looked unfamiliar or strange to him. Willing to at least try the new food, he put the wafer in his mouth and began to chew. A biting, soapy flavor assaulted his tasted buds, and he immediately spewed the offensive morsel back into his hand. Jacob sat spitting and sputtering, trying to clear his mouth of the horrible taste.

He realized his antics had drawn the attention of the Englishman sitting beside him. Embarrassed and defensive he said, "Well, what kind of food is this anyway?"

The Englishman burst into laughter so hearty, he turned bright red. Jacob was beginning to worry the man would wheeze himself to death when he finally began to collect himself. "It's a handi-wipe," he explained. "You wipe your hands with it when you've finished the meal."

Jacob burned with embarrassment. Of all the items on his plate, he'd managed to eat the only inedible one. He returned to his meal and, to his relief, finished eating without further catastrophes.

Several hours later, the plane landed in Amsterdam, Holland, the airplane's layover stop. Jacob leaned toward the small window, eager to have his first look at snow. A layer of downy white coated everything in sight, creating a scene unlike anything Jacob had viewed before that moment. He couldn't wait to go outside and touch the snow, explore it with his hands and senses.

While they waited for the airport personnel to finish the landing procedures, Jacob watched the ground crew approach the plane, preparing to offload the luggage stored in the cargo hold beneath the passenger cabin. As they went about their work, soft white clouds billowed from their mouths.

"The people in Holland must all be smokers," Jacob commented to the Englishman next to him.

A look of confusion passed over the man's face. "Why do you say that?"

"Look at the ground crew," Jacob said. "Each time they open their mouths a cloud of smoke comes out."

The Englishman again burst into laughter. He shook and wheezed for several minutes before he calmed enough to talk. "When a person's warm, moist breath meets the cold air, it produces a cloud. You will blow smoke too when you step outside."

Jacob was doubtful, but he decided to keep quiet, figuring his ignorance had provided the Englishman with enough entertainment for one day.

When the passengers received permission to disembark, Jacob rose and walked down the stairs the ground crew had placed alongside the plane. Eager to touch the snow, Jacob stooped down and tried to gather up a handful of the white substance. But as he leaned over, his shoes slipped out from under him, and he landed on his face with a thud. The Englishman's chuckle sounded beside him, and Jacob felt himself lifted out of the snow. Several passengers and crew tried to set him back on his feet, but the soles of Jacob's shoes were too smooth, and he only slipped again. Taking pity on the poor Nigerian, they half-carried, half-dragged him into the airport, sharing yet another laugh at his expense.

And so began the first of many new experiences and challenges he would face as he entered a new country to live among a people and culture very different from his own.

• • •

After the long and difficult journey, Jacob arrived at Emmanuel Bible College in Ontario, Canada. He immediately discovered that Canada and Amsterdam had something in common—snow. Jacob's earlier fascination with the snow had vanished, driven away the instant he tumbled face first into the cold, white substance. In addition, he was learning that living in Nigeria, where temperatures average more than one hundred degrees in the shade, had not prepared him to deal with such cold temperatures. Just before Jacob left Nigeria, Art Reifel had given him a sports coat, insisting he would need it. While Jacob was grateful for the extra layer of clothing, it was not adequate to keep him warm. Each time he went outdoors, Jacob rushed back inside, teeth chattering and skin covered in goose bumps.

Jacob stayed in his dorm room for two weeks, afraid he would die from exposure to the cold and snow. From time to time, his roommate came and dragged him out under protest, forcing him to go to the cafeteria and classes. Jacob's dorm mates found his aversion to snow very amusing. They brought snowballs back to the room and slipped them under his pillow to tease him. Eventually, Jacob's Nigerian blood adjusted to the cold Canadian winter temperatures, and he settled into the routine of classes and study.

Because he had transferred credits from Ilorin and because he went to school year-round, Jacob was able to graduate within a year. He left Emmanuel with two diplomas, one in Theology and the other in Christian

Education. These qualified him to teach in the Christian institutions of Nigeria.

In 1967, Jacob returned to Ilorin, this time as a teacher and assistant principal to John Bontrager. He reunited with his family and brought them all to Ilorin, including his aunt Apalu. Near the campus, the Bawas found a house adequate for their growing family. Jacob quickly settled into the familiar routine at Ilorin, though this time he was leading the class rather than sitting in it. He taught daily, his curriculum consisting of mostly Bible courses. Occasionally, the school assigned him a class in sociology, geography, Nigerian history or other social science courses.

• • •

As a talented man with a willingness to serve, Jacob received several job offers, not all from the Missionary Church. When the government heard Jacob had returned to Nigeria, they offered him a position at the Government Teacher's College. "We need someone to teach Christian Religious Knowledge (CRK) to college students training to become teachers. Would you be interested in this position?"

The government required all teachers-in-training to take either Christian Religious Knowledge or Islamic Religious Knowledge as part of their college studies. Jacob could not decline the opportunity to teach unsaved teachers about Jesus. So three times a week, he went into town to teach CRK.

As one of Ilorin's male staff members, Jacob occasionally preached a Sunday sermon at the College Chapel. However, he concentrated the larger part of his ministry efforts on the Hausa Police Church. Many members of his former congregation remembered Jacob from his college days, and they welcomed him back into a leadership role at the assembly.

Jacob also accepted the title of Manager of the Missionary Schools in Nigeria. He performed the administrative duties that kept the Missionary schools funded, staffed and supplied. After a short time in this role, the Nigerian government assumed responsibility for all the Christian schools and their functioning. Jacob then turned his efforts to helping Rose found the United Missionary Theological College Chapel School, a primary school run on Ilorin's campus. Rose and Mrs. Olaniya, who had earned a college degree in early childhood education, opened a nursery class. After establishing a few classes, the school added kindergarten and primary grades as they were able to fund and staff more classrooms.

Throughout his time at Ilorin, Jacob continued to serve in multiple roles, freely giving his time and energy to teach, minister, and further the gospel in any way he could. God blessed the work of Jacob's hands and helped him to accomplish an amazing amount of work in the twenty-four hours he had each day.

• • •

The school at Ilorin was hosting a big conference on evangelism and had invited pastors from different parts of Nigeria to attend. Because of Jacob's skill with languages, conference planners asked him to interpret for the speakers who came from the United States. Jacob accepted the task of translating the English messages into Hausa for those Nigerians who did not understand English.

One of the speakers for whom Jacob translated was an African-American man from Ohio who worked with d/Deaf youth. The young man, who was d/Deaf himself, communicated primarily through sign language. The Nigerians had never seen people speak with their hands and found the display very amusing. They watched with fascination, grinning and sometimes chuckling at what they perceived to be antics on the speaker's part.

Jacob had never witnessed this form of communication, yet he was expected to interpret for this speaker. In addition to signing, the young man was able to verbalize the words, though his pronunciation was not entirely clear. Jacob struggled with the different accents and pronunciations stemming from their varied origins and methods of communication.

Jacob and the speaker struggled through the first few minutes of the sermon, both men fumbling to understand and be understood. Then Jacob realized if he watched the man's lips, his eyes could understand the English words much easier than his ears. After that moment, Jacob translated with little trouble until the man mentioned snow. Somehow, that frustrating word always hindered Jacob's translation efforts.

Jacob's friends were incredibly impressed, even those who spoke some English. "How did you understand what the man was saying?" they asked.

Jacob recognized God's grace, which allowed him to perform a task he could not have otherwise done.

• • •

In the middle of a service, someone came and tapped Jacob on the shoulder. "You must come quickly," they said. "You are needed at home."

"What happened?" Jacob asked, wondering what could be so urgent that they would try to pull him away from his translating duties.

"Rose is in labor! You must come and drive her to the hospital." Jacob's wife, who was nearing the end of another pregnancy, had chosen an inconvenient time to deliver. Jacob was one of the few people qualified to translate at this large conference. If he left, the speakers would not have an adequate translator, and hundreds of ministers would not understand the messages.

"I can't just leave," he said, torn between love for his wife and child and his responsibility to the conference. After some deliberation, Jacob approached one of the missionaries and asked them to take charge of Rose's care. They agreed Jacob should stay at the conference and promptly left to drive Rose to the maternity hospital.

Though anxious for news, Jacob stayed to the end of the conference. As soon as he was able, he rushed to the hospital. He found his wife and newborn son in good health and ready to forgive him for missing the birth. Rose and Jacob named their son Timothy Taruwa (a Hausa word meaning meeting or conference) Bawa.

• • •

Several months after Timothy's birth, the baby and the Bawa's pet monkey clashed. The Bawas had hired a housegirl to watch the children and perform basic chores while Jacob and Rose tended to their ministerial duties. The young woman always carried Timothy in a sling on her back. Timothy liked the sling and usually fell asleep in his carrier.

During that time, the Bawas owned a pet monkey. The animal was tied outside the house where the children could visit and play with it outdoors. One day, the babysitter stopped to play with the monkey. As she talked to it and teased it, the animal became very irate. "Stop that!" she scolded. "What is wrong with you, little monkey?"

It screamed and jumped and wildly waved its hands through the air. The more she tried to pacify the monkey, the more vicious it became.

Bewildered by the monkey's strange behavior, the babysitter turned to walk away. As she did, the animal leapt onto her back and clawed at the baby, managing to give Timothy's cheek a deep cut before it let go. Frantic, she ran for help, and a neighbor rushed her and the baby to the hospital, where Timothy received several stitches.

When Jacob heard the news, he hurried to the hospital, worried about his infant son. By the time he arrived, Timothy's cheek had been stitched and bandaged. Thankful the wound was not life-threatening, Jacob escorted his family and housegirl home.

Later, a neighbor told the Bawas that monkeys are very jealous creatures. When they see a baby riding on a person's back, they can hardly contain their agitation and are known to lash out at the child. From then on, the Bawas and the housegirl kept the baby away from the monkey. Timothy's cut eventually healed, though he still bears a scar from the incident.

• • •

In 1969, while Jacob served at Ilorin, one of his former teachers—Naomi Everett—joined the staff as an English teacher. Though they hadn't seen one another for several years, they easily resumed their friendship, this time as colleagues and friends rather than teacher and student. They spent many hours sitting in Naomi's living room or on the veranda steps discussing God's plans for their lives. Both were facing monumental changes.

Shortly after arriving at Ilorin, Naomi had been asked to take a position as principal of a new high school the Missionary Church intended to open at Tungan Magajiya, where Rose's parents were stationed at the time. Jacob was anticipating another trip to the United States, where he hoped to further his education. They would leave Ilorin's campus at the same time, heading in different directions.

The months they spent on Ilorin's campus passed quickly, and they prepared to go their separate ways again. Before they parted company, Jacob offered Naomi some appreciated assistance. When word about the new school spread, more than nine hundred prospective students came to take the entrance exam, but the school had class space for only thirty-six. From the pool of nine hundred, the students with the top one hundred fifty scores were interviewed. Naomi had no staff and no one to help her with the selection process. Jacob volunteered to travel with her across the mission territory, stopping in several locations to conduct the many interviews.

Not only was Naomi grateful for his help and opinion in the matter, she also appreciated his prayerful insight and Nigerian perspective. The educational system in 1960s Nigeria was underdeveloped. The government and missionary schools had limited classroom space, and only a small percentage of children who wanted education could actually obtain one.

Naomi approached the student selection process with great serious-ness, knowing the decisions she and Jacob made would be one of the most important in the lives of the young applicants. God's hand was upon the selections. After she and Jacob filled the thirty-six spaces, Naomi went on to teach a wonderful group of students.

Because Jacob was leaving, Rose traveled back to Tungan Magajiya to live near her parents. In addition to caring for her five children, she worked with Naomi Everett, serving as dorm matron to the young ladies who boarded at the new U.M.S. school.

10

Chapter Ten

Bethel, Emmanuel and Trinity

"Father, I am going back to the United States. I will be leaving the country soon." Jacob sat down beside his father, intending to say goodbye.

"What are you going to do there?"

"I am continuing my education."

"Aren't you tired of studying yet? You are becoming a professional student. When are you going to settle down and work?" A simple man who loved the land, Bagudu had never understood Jacob's passion for learning.

Jacob smiled at his father. "When I come back to Nigeria, I will put all my learning to good use." Jacob paused, drawing a deep breath and summoning his courage. "Before I go, I want to address a concern with you."

His father nodded. "Go ahead."

"I want very much to see you come to the saving knowledge of the Lord Jesus Christ." Jacob held his breath, praying for a good outcome to the conversation.

"You and your wife and children are Christians. I keep telling you that when I die, God will put me wherever you are. He will show me mercy for your sake."

"No, Father, there will be no mercy. You have been to church with us, and we have shared the gospel with you in our home. You know the way of salvation. You must choose Jesus for yourself. My choice cannot save you."

"I will think about it." Bagudu changed the subject, and the men talked of other issues for a time. Eventually, the conversation returned to matters of faith.

"Let me be firm with you," Bagudu said. "I do not want to become a Christian because I am afraid. I am a tribal leader, and my conversion will cause conflict with the chief. I would rather wait until you come back. Perhaps then I will feel ready to believe."

"You never know what could happen," Jacob pleaded, clinging to hope. "I will be away for two years."

Bagudu waved his hand, dismissing the possibility of tragedy. "All will be well. You will see."

A weight of disappointment settled into Jacob's chest. Knowing his father's mind was set, Jacob honored the decision and said no more.

• • •

When Jacob returned to North America in 1971, he left his family behind in Tungan Magajiya with Rose's parents. The months after his departure proved to be a painful time of separation for them all. Each morning as Rose and the children had their devotions, Rose reminded the children to pray for their baba (daddy). "He is in a different country, called Canada," she reminded them.

James, who missed his father terribly, burst into tears and became almost feverish with distress when he thought about his father being away. "Why did God take our daddy to another place without us? Tell Jesus to send him back!" James demanded.

Rose had her hands full caring for five children who missed their father very much. Rose and Jacob also felt the separation deeply. After a year, the mission board decided Rose should go to Canada to stay with Jacob so the married couple could be together. However, this meant Rose had to leave the children behind with her parents.

"I don't think I can do it," she told Jacob. "It will be hard for me to leave them and difficult for my parents at their age to care for five children. And Timothy is still so young."

But when Rose's parents heard the mission board's suggestions, they urged her to go. "A wife should be with her husband. We can handle the children," they assured her.

• • •

Rose was restless in Canada. Accustomed to caring for their children and also working in the ministry, the absence of activity in Canada disturbed her. She also worried about the baby and her mother's ability to care for such a young child. When Rose learned that her sister had sent three children to live at their parents' home, putting a total of eight children in the older couple's care, she pleaded to fly home. But at the same time, she knew that if she went to Nigeria to be with her children, she would suffer the separation from Jacob. Caught in a no-win situation, she stayed in Canada.

Jacob finished his Bachelor's of Theology in Biblical Studies in 1972 then moved on to Bethel College, Indiana, for several semesters. He needed to add some liberal arts credits to his transcript, and Bethel offered a wide variety of classes from which to choose.

In 1974, Jacob enrolled in Trinity International University, Illinois, where he studied for his Master's in Education with an emphasis on guidance and counseling, areas of training which would help him fulfill his role as a leader at Ilorin when the time came.

• • •

During his stay at Trinity, Jacob received a heartbreaking telegram.

"Jacob, your father was killed. Can you return home?"

Jacob slumped into a chair, the memories of his final conversation with his father playing through his mind. Had Bagudu turned to God before his untimely death? Jacob hoped so.

Jacob phoned the headquarters in Fort Wayne and told them about his loss and requested permission to return home for a short time to pay his respects and grieve his father's death. The mission board agreed, and Jacob went to the dean of students at Trinity and told him of his plans to return to Nigeria for a time.

"What about Rose?" the dean asked. "Aren't you taking her with you?"

Jacob shook his head. "I can only afford one ticket. Rose will have to stay here."

The dean looked pensive for a moment. "It would not be good for you to go alone."

Later the dean phoned. "Someone has given us money for a ticket, so you can take Rose to see the children." A medical doctor who heard about Jacob's loss had offered to sponsor the trip. The Bawas packed their bags and flew to Nigeria.

• • •

Jacob sat in the family compound, listening to his cousins tell the story surrounding Bagudu's death. Several men had been drinking in a compound up the road. They argued and four men ganged up against one. Frightened, the man ran down the road, slipped inside Jacob's family's compound and hid himself. The four men chased him and stormed inside the compound. They found Bagudu sitting on a mat, playing with his cousin's baby.

"Where is he?" they yelled, fury burning in their bloodshot eyes.

"Who?" Bagudu asked, standing to his feet and facing the men who had intruded on his family's quiet evening.

"Somebody insulted us and ran into this compound. We are sure he came in here. Where is he?"

Bagudu shook his head. "I have been sitting here all evening. I saw no one come inside. Perhaps you are mistaken." The women sitting near Bagudu nodded their agreement. They had seen no one enter.

"You are not telling us the truth!" The men pounced upon Bagudu, beating him and knocking him to the ground. One of the drunken men pulled out a large knife and plunged it into Bagudu's chest. A dark red stain of blood soaked through his clothes and spilled onto the ground. As quickly as they'd come, the men fled into the shadowed streets and disappeared.

Bagudu's family rushed to his aid, tending his wounds to the best of their ability and trying to make him comfortable. Someone ran for the missionary, and the man offered to drive Bagudu to the hospital thirty miles away. Several of Bagudu's cousins loaded him into the missionary's vehicle, and the small group made a desperate journey in the dark of night. Before they arrived at the hospital, Bagudu passed from this world.

Jacob felt a heaviness in his heart as he listened to the tale. His father had been a strong man who would have lived many years if not for this tragic occurrence. With no way of knowing the condition of his father's heart, Jacob could only hope Bagudu had embraced salvation before his death.

• • •

After spending time in Salka and paying their final respects to his father, Jacob and Rose traveled to Tungan Magajiya to see the children. When they walked into the compound, their older children ran to their side and lavished hugs and kisses on them.

"Mama, Baba, we've missed you!" they cried. Soon, tears appeared in the children's eyes, and they asked, "Why did you leave us for such a long time? Why did you not take us with you?"

Jacob and Rose had missed their children dearly and felt guilty when they realized how much the separation had impacted the older children. However, baby Timothy dealt them the worst blow. Rose, eager to hold her little one, held out her arms to Timothy and said, "Mama is here. Come to Mama."

Timothy stared at her with wide, fearful eyes and ran to hide behind his grandmother's skirts. Because he'd been so young when they left him, Timothy could not remember his parents and viewed them as strangers. At the same time, he'd grown very fond of his grandmother. While the older children attended school or played with friends, Timothy spent his days toddling around the house behind his grandmother, watching her work. He made it clear that he loved his grandmother and wanted nothing to do with his parents.

Rose cried for days, feeling as if she'd somehow failed her children. Finally, after three weeks of wooing and coaxing, little Timothy warmed to Jacob and Rose and accepted their affection. But after six weeks at her parents' home, Jacob and Rose had to return to the United States to finish the term at Trinity International University.

Rose cried, and the children cried, dreading another time of separation. While the Bawas recognized that God wanted them to increase their education and prepare them for ministry, they admit this sacrifice was one of the most difficult they have ever made.

11

Chapter Eleven

Magiro Exposed

After completing his Master's in Christian Education in 1974, Jacob returned to Nigeria to serve as vice-principal of Ilorin Theological Seminary and Associate Pastor of the Chapel. The board and the college principal, John Bontrager, made it clear that Jacob was being groomed to assume leadership of the school.

Several profound incidents took place during Jacob's term at the college, one of which brought drastic change to Salka and its residents.

• • •

During December of each year, the Magiro worshippers (men only) of Salka, Nigeria, would gather together for a seven-day festival. During this time, the dragon-god frequently roamed the streets of the village, so the fearful women stayed hidden inside their homes. Normally, this festival offered the men and older boys an excuse to eat, drink, and revel in the open without interference from their wives and mothers. But in 1974 the festival progressed much differently than usual.

The village of Salka consists of five large family units living in close proximity. While each family lived in their own compound, the entire village participated in the Magiro worship together and submitted to the headship of one chief.

Prior to the 1974 festival, the head blacksmith in Salka died. Each of the families in Salka had a blacksmith. The title of "head blacksmith" was bestowed by the chief and considered a great and coveted honor. Normally, the privilege was rotated among the five sections of town, allowing each family the honor of the title in turn. This time, the chief was expected to choose the head blacksmith from the Ketarin Daji family, as it was their turn.

But, in an uncharacteristic deviation from the routine, the chief appointed a blacksmith from the same family as the one who had just died. The people of Ketarin Daji were furious.

"We have been robbed of the honor due to us!"

"The chief does not respect us. He is not a fair leader."

"Let us abandon this chief and rule ourselves," someone suggested. The Ketarin Daji men discussed the matter and agreed. They no longer wished to submit to Salka's chief, so they withdrew from the village and turned their backs on its leader. The men appointed a family member as their chief and established a governing system independent of their former connections to Salka.

Shortly afterward, the time for the December Magiro festival arrived. Most of the men from Ketarin Daji boycotted the festivities held in Salka. However, ten men chose to go, ignoring the advice of their family members to stay away. When they arrived at the festival, the men from the other families taunted them. "What are you doing here? We thought you said you didn't want to belong with us any more."

The men of Ketarin Daji replied, "We want to have our share in Magiro too."

Angered, the men from the rest of the town ganged up on the ten men from Ketarin Daji. Outnumbered, the men of Ketarin Daji received a terrible beating, and one man died. The survivors returned to their family compound and reported the incident to the rest of the family. Enraged, the men of Ketarin Daji gathered guns, bows and axes and came against the men who had killed their brother and beaten their family members. After a night of fierce fighting and bloodshed, governmental authorities came and restored the peace.

But the men of Ketarin Daji had not finished with their revenge. Disillusioned with Magiro, they brought out the flutes, drums and iron rings and showed their women the secrets of Magiro. They explained everything, admitting all their deceit to the women. Like anywhere else in the world, Salka's women like to talk and gossip. The Ketarin Daji women told the secrets to the women in the other families, and soon the entire village knew the truth. Magiro was a sham. Many declared they would have nothing more to do with their pagan religion. One dark night, someone set fire to Magiro's hut in the center of town. Magiro's dwelling burned to the ground, and no one bothered to rebuild it.

Some villagers of Salka practiced another form of pagan worship called Agunu. Shortly after the trouble within the Magiro sect, another part of the population pulled out of the Agunu cult and also denounced their pagan beliefs. The cult members were usually loyal to one another, but the Agunu leader's son stole the fiancée of another member. The betrayal caused a rebellion. The section to which the wronged man belonged said the incident proved Agunu was not a true religion.

Almost overnight, thousands of people had denounced their false religions, leaving a tremendous religious vacuum in the town. Muslims stepped in, attempting to convert the former pagans to Islam, but the Christians also seized the opportunity. They knew God had sown confusion into the enemy's camp and was working to turn the hearts of the Kambari to Him.

• • •

A group of Salka's men sought out Pastor Ibrahim Langashi, a Salka native who had been through the Hausa Bible School training and now served as pastor to the town.

"Pasto, Pasto, will you help us find the Jesus way?" they asked.

Pastor Ibrahim and the Christians in the community quickly found themselves overwhelmed with seekers and new converts. The harvest was ripe, but the laborers too few. Not wanting to allow the opportunity to slip through their fingers, they sent word to Ilorin Theological Seminary requesting a team of evangelists and ministers come to Salka to help them fill the Kambari's religious void with the good news of Jesus Christ.

Jacob rejoiced to hear that God had answered one of his most fervent prayers—to free his people from the bondage of Magiro worship. He quickly assembled a team of a dozen men to help with the work in Salka. They held camp meetings and organized evangelistic efforts, trying to reach every Kambari person with the gospel.

Every member of the church in Salka had been trained to do personal evangelism through the New Life for All program, which Jacob implemented during his pastorship there. Because the Kambari were hungry for answers and because of the large number of people performing evangelistic work, the Christian church in Salka multiplied rapidly.

Almost overnight, the church population more than doubled in one year. Each of the five families in Salka wanted their own place of worship, so the people built a church in each section of Salka. The buildings filled immediately.

After Salka's revival, the evangelistic efforts spread to other towns and cities. People gave their hearts to the Lord by the hundreds and volunteered to build a church in their own cities. The missionaries who had labored in the field for nearly half a century were finally reaping a bountiful harvest.

12

Chapter Twelve

Promotion from Above

During Jacob's term as vice-principal of Ilorin Theological Seminary, members of the school board decided to work toward transforming Ilorin into an accredited college that could offer degree programs approved by the Nigerian government. In order to take that step, the government required a Nigerian national to sit at the head of the college, and that person would need to have a doctorate degree. Jacob was selected to return to the United States to continue his education.

He researched various universities and decided to attend Michigan State University because of its strong education program. In addition, he had heard of a professor named Dr. Ted Ward who was a strong Christian and well-known Bible scholar. Dr. Ward had been involved in theological education by extension, a program Jacob was interested in implementing in Nigeria. Dr. Ward was working in the education department. Hoping to find a mentor in this man he admired, Jacob requested Dr. Ward as his advisor. His request was granted.

In September of 1975, Jacob and his family moved to East Lansing, Michigan. Unlike his first few trips to the United States, this time Jacob brought his entire family. The older children, Grace, James and Sarah, attended Lansing High School, while the younger ones, Timmy and Jerry, went to elementary and junior high schools. All the children had studied

English at the U.M.S. schools in Nigeria, so they already had a good grasp of the language. Studying in the United States only solidified their English skills, and soon they talked like native Americans.

While the children attended school, Rose studied early childhood education at Lansing Community College. She had worked in classrooms for many years as a nursery school teacher and decided she wanted to obtain a degree which would allow her to work in Nigeria's public school system when they returned home. Having taken classes at many of the institutions Jacob attended through the years, Rose had already fulfilled several semesters of her degree requirements.

During Jacob's first semester at the university, he earned a grade point average of 4.0, which qualified him to be a graduate assistant. Someone on the university staff asked him if he would like to have a part-time job marking papers, giving exams, and occasionally teaching a class in African studies or filling in for absent instructors. Jacob accepted the position, which provided extra spending money for his family and also gave him a look behind the scenes at how the administration operated at Michigan State.

Jacob worked hard at his studies, and within one semester had earned his second master's degree, this one in education. He then continued toward his Ph.D. in Curriculum and Instruction. To his delight, Dr. Ward served as the chairman of his dissertation committee and spent many hours mentoring Jacob in his studies. Jacob and Dr. Ward got along well, making Jacob's time of study at Michigan State a pleasure.

• • •

After Jacob acquired his Ph.D., the university offered him a position as an instructor. He and Rose discussed the offer and decided it would be good to stay on for a year. Their older children were scheduled to graduate from high school in one year, and it seemed wise to keep them in the same school and country rather than uproot them so close to finishing.

Michigan State University placed Jacob in the department of Oriental and African studies in linguistics. He taught classes in Hausa and the methodology of learning a language in a different culture.

• • •

While Jacob was still in the United States, the leaders of the Missionary Church in Nigeria decided the time had come to place the leadership of the church into the hands of the Nigerians. After fifty years of evangelism, teaching, and training, the Nigerians were prepared and equipped to assume responsibility for the churches and missionary works in their country. While the missionaries would stay to assist, they would now answer to the Nigerians rather than leading them.

At the general conference, a committee discussed the matter and put the issue to a vote. In the end, they elected Jacob to serve as President of the United Missionary Church of Africa (U.M.C.A.). Jacob, who was still in the United States, was not present at the vote. Several weeks later, he received a letter in the mail informing him that when he returned to Nigeria, the Missionary organization wanted him to serve as President.

In 1979, when Rose had finished her college degree and his three oldest children had graduated from Lansing High School, Jacob moved his family back to Ilorin, where U.M.C.A. headquarters were situated not far from the seminary campus. Jacob quickly adapted to his new administrative role, planning conferences, counseling pastors, dealing with denominational problems, traveling to speak at meetings in various parts of the country, and visiting the churches under his jurisdiction.

His job proved so demanding that Rose did not attempt to find a teaching position. She divided her time between the responsibilities of her home and entertaining the guests that arrived unannounced at headquarters on a daily basis.

Since Jacob's three older children had graduated from high school in the United States, they were now ready to proceed to college. Sarah chose to attend Ahmadu Bello University to pursue theater arts, in addition to English and French studies. James enrolled in Nigerian Television College to pursue his journalism interests. Grace also began in a journalism program but later switched to banking. Jerry and Timmy, the younger two children, continued their secondary education in Ilorin.

13

Chapter Thirteen

Spreading the Good News

In 1980, the Niger State government decided Christian Religious Knowledge (CRK) classes should be implemented in all of Niger State's primary and secondary schools. Until that time, Islamic Religious Knowledge was a required course, but the interests of the growing Christian population had been ignored. While some teachers had studied the Christian religion as part of their college training, CRK had not been implemented in public school classrooms. Public demand for Christian training increased to the extent that officials could no longer ignore it.

Government officials began searching for someone qualified to establish a state-wide program. Jacob's background in both education and theology made him an attractive candidate for the job. They approached him with an offer, but Jacob was reluctant to accept. He had only just begun his term as president of the U.M.C.A. and was not sure it was God's will for him to leave that position already. He agreed to consider the matter and pray about it.

When the United Missionary Church heard about the offer, they encouraged Jacob to grab it. "This is an opportunity to minister the gospel in every Niger State public school! And you would have the authority to shape and influence how the program is taught. Take the position, Jacob. We feel God's hand is behind the offer."

So with the church's blessing, Jacob accepted the government job and moved to Minna. Working under the title of Chief Inspector of Education, Ministry of Education, Niger State Public Schools, he wrote curriculum and developed a program for staff recruitment and training. He quickly realized Nigeria lacked teachers with backgrounds in Bible knowledge. Despite an aggressive recruitment campaign, the applicants were few. Regardless of the teacher shortage, the state wanted the positions filled. Jacob could not fill the positions in the schools the traditional way.

To meet the demand, he turned to the clergy. If a pastor of an established church lived near a school, Jacob contacted the church leader and asked him to come for an interview with the board. If the board felt the man was qualified and if the pastor were willing, he was given the responsibility of teaching the Christian Religious Knowledge curriculum in the public school five days a week. The Ministry of Education paid the church for the service, and pastors drew new members to their congregations, creating a beneficial arrangement for all involved.

Even after employing pastors, Jacob needed more teachers. He created a budget for the department, proposing that the government pay for people to attend Bible college or seminary in order to train to become CRK teachers. The government agreed to offer full scholarships to anyone willing to teach CRK in the public school system.

Jacob began accepting applications and sending people to Ilorin Theological Seminary, Baptist Seminary, and Sudan Interior Mission Seminary. Within a few years, qualified CRK teachers staffed the public schools. The government was so impressed with Jacob's accomplishments they asked him to develop a training program for army chaplains, as well. Jacob agreed and began staffing the army with Christian leadership.

In addition to staffing the CRK classes and army chaplains, Jacob was responsible for overseeing the entire Niger State school system from kindergarten through the college level, all of which were under the government's jurisdiction. Jacob or one of the inspectors who answered to him inspected and approved any plans to build private schools or colleges, insuring they met with government standards and regulations.

Once again, God had prepared Jacob with experience and education then opened a door of opportunity. And with God's hand of blessing upon his life, he excelled at his work, impacting thousands of lives with the gospel.

• • •

Because of his outstanding work as the Chief Inspector of Education, Jacob received a promotion to the position of Permanent Secretary of Education. In this role Jacob answered to the Commissioner of the Ministry of Education who answered to the State Governor. Eventually, the Niger State Governor promoted Jacob by also appointing him to serve as the Commissioner of the Ministry of Health. This position is equivalent to an appointment to serve as one of the Governor's cabinet members in the United States.

As the Commissioner of the Ministry of Health, Jacob ensured that every local government area had an adequate number of clinics and hospitals. When a new facility was raised or when a position opened, Jacob appointed medical officers to head the new medical facilities. Though this position did not correlate with Jacob's educational background and area of expertise, he enjoyed it. The position was largely administrative, and if an issue arose that required medical expertise, Jacob called on one of the many doctors and medical personnel under his jurisdiction to advise him.

After three months in the Ministry of Health, a vacancy opened back in the Education department. The man the government had hoped to appoint as Commissioner for the Ministry of Education was continuing his education at Howard University. The government needed someone to fill an interim position, so they asked Jacob to serve in that capacity until the man's return. Jacob tried to decline the position in the Ministry of Education, unsure how he would manage to head both departments effectively. Because of Jacob's education and obvious qualifications, the government refused to take no for an answer. So, Jacob found himself with two full-time jobs.

• • •

Another part of Jacob's job involved training people to fill roles at both the Ministry of Education and the Ministry of Health. In some instances a person only needed to attend a seminar or apprentice for a time in order to prepare for a new position. But sometimes a person needed to return to college to earn a higher degree. In these instances, the Nigerian government was usually willing to pay for a government employee's education. Staff members desiring to return to school filled out request forms and sent them to Jacob. If Jacob approved, the staff member would be sent to school while the government continued to pay the student a full salary in addition to an allowance, which covered the cost of tuition, books and moderate spending.

• • •

In 1984, Jacob added to his governmental responsibilities. He was asked to represent Niger State on the board of the United Bank of Africa. The appointment required attendance at monthly meetings, travel, and recruitment of bankers from around the world. The United Bank of Africa had affiliated banks in other countries, which included London, England, and Paris, France. The Board often traveled to Europe to study the administration and organizational structure of sister banks.

Since, the board members were encouraged to bring their spouses, Rose was able to accompany Jacob on his travels. When the board members gathered to meet, the spouses planned an outing together, usually shopping, a tour, or dinner at a restaurant.

As a board member, Jacob helped to govern and administrate the United Bank of Africa. The board selected high-ranking personnel to run Nigeria's financial institutions and implemented new policies and procedures in addition to solving problems. While Jacob enjoyed the task, he sometimes worked from 7:30 a.m. to 1:00 a.m. the next day. This in addition to his two full-time jobs at the Ministries of Health and Education kept him incredibly busy.

• • •

In 1984, after completing his training at the National Institute, the Nigerian University Commission asked Jacob to move to Minna and serve as Registrar at the Federal University of Technology. The university was organizing their curriculum and study programs and needed someone with Jacob's experience and expertise to help administrate. Jacob suspected the government had placed him there for reasons other than the obvious ones. Many men and women sent to work at the Federal University were later promoted into the highest levels of government service. Jacob wondered if he was being considered for a big promotion.

He had served as Nigeria's Acting Chairman of the Scholarship Board, a federal commission which determined the requirements for the various degree programs in the country's universities, so he was an ideal candidate to help structure the academic programs at a new university. With Jacob's help, the school opened with seven thousand students. He spent three years at the university.

• • •

In 1985, Jacob received a letter, offering him one of the most prestigious honors Nigeria can extend to a citizen. The president of Nigeria invited him to attend the National Institute for Policy and Strategic Studies (N.I.P.S.S.). The invitation took Jacob by surprise. He knew the president extended these invitations to Nigeria's elite, usually persons the government intended to place in positions of authority in the future. While Jacob had successfully served the government and steadily advanced his career, he did not expect to be nominated for such an honor.

When the appointed time came, Jacob moved to the city of Kuru (a small town near Jos) to sit in a class of ninety people from the military, police, navy, air force, and other government servants from the civilian population like Jacob. His classmates consisted of eighty-nine men and one woman.

The nine-month program, which still operates today, is tailored for top policy makers and executives from all walks of Nigerian national life. N.I.P.S.S. serves as an intellectual support for people charged with the responsibility of formulating and implementing policies and development strategies for the country. Students sit in seminars and workshops about national and global issues then conduct interdisciplinary research on all sectors of Nigerian life.

The school invites ambassadors from countries around the world to come and speak about issues affecting the world. Speakers are given immunity to speak freely in the confidential classes. Many sensitive issues are discussed openly. Students are expected to take notes and are given exams on the materials covered by the speakers and discussions.

At the end of the nine-month term, each student writes and presents a thesis. Their theses and reports are disseminated in the forms of books, monographs and reports, which are widely circulated within and outside government circles. So N.I.P.S.S. serves as both training ground and innovative think tank for future governmental policies and procedures. After students successfully complete the nine-months of classroom study, they receive the M.N.I. status (Member National Institute), one of the highest honors a Nigerian can receive.

Jacob was thrilled to be included in the stimulating program and was honored to be counted among Nigeria's elite. After the nine-month classroom study, the ninety students divided into nine syndicates, or groups, and began a tour. Jacob's group spent three months visiting ten African countries to study their governmental structures and various systems in the country, such as the educational system, banking system, and medical system. The group elected a secretary to keep notes of all they learned and how they might use that knowledge to improve Nigeria's methods in these areas.

After the tour of Africa, the group returned to the school and presented their findings to the school board. The board found their report satisfactory and advanced them to the next phase of the project—a three-month world tour to countries outside of the African continent. The board assigned Jacob's group to visit Japan, Russia, Austria, England, and the United States. Once again the ten members of the syndicate packed their bags and boarded a plane to Japan, the first stop on the itinerary.

The Japanese government had graciously agreed to host the visiting Nigerians during their 1986 visit. Shortly after Jacob's plane landed, his group received a message that the emperor had planned a large banquet in their honor. They were to report to the emperor's palace the following evening, where they would meet the emperor, the prime minister and many top-ranking Japanese government officials. Jacob and his peers were honored to receive such a cordial welcome.

The following evening they dressed in their finest baban rigas (big gowns), the traditional garment of the Nigerians, in which a long-sleeved tunic is worn over long pants. The ensemble also includes an elaborately embroidered hat, which takes an elderly Nigerian woman approximately three months to sew by hand.

As soon as they arrived at the palace, introductions began. They met many of Japan's leaders in addition to ambassadors from other countries. Japan's emperor and prime minister were among the crowd of five hundred people.

After a cocktail hour, the emperor's guests were escorted to the banquet hall and were given seats at the head table along the front of the room. After the banquet room had filled, the Chief of Protocol approached Jacob's group with some instructions. "You and the members of your group are to visit the food table first. If you will follow me, I will show you the way." He turned and led them toward a table spread with food unfamiliar to the Nigerians.

A geisha dressed in a beautiful kimono appeared at their side and bowed to Jacob and his peers. "You are to start here and fill a plate with food," she explained through a translator. She pointed at one particular dish and said in halting English, "Nice. Very good."

Jacob thanked her, and being polite, filled his plate with the dish she had recommended. He returned to the head table and sat. Eager to experience the new and interesting food on his plate, he took a bite of the food the geisha had suggested. The flavor assaulted his taste buds, and he did not like it at all. He gulped his water to wash away the taste and stared at the heaping mound on his plate, suddenly sorry he had taken such a large portion of the dish. He pondered the dilemma a moment and decided it would be rude not to eat it. Not wanting to offend his hosts, he resigned himself to drinking plenty of water to wash down the food.

Dutifully, he took another bite followed by another swallow of water. After several more bites, his stomach began to groan and churn. He clutched at his stomach, painfully aware of the embarrassing noises his body was making. Thinking more water might calm his stomach, Jacob took another drink. To his dismay, he only felt worse. Sickening nausea gripped him, and Jacob realized that the food he'd ingested was not going to stay down. He needed to find a restroom immediately!

To Jacob's misfortune, he could not simply leave the head table and run through the nearest door. One does not wander aimlessly about the emperor's palace looking for a restroom. Jacob turned in his chair and signaled to the geisha, hoping she could direct him to the appropriate doorway. When he caught her attention, he beckoned to her with a wave of his hand.

"I'm coming," she said. "One moment."

Unaware of the severity of Jacob's situation, the geisha continued to perform her hostess duties, taking her time in coming to his aid. Jacob suffered in silence for nearly fifteen minutes, clutching his raging stomach and swallowing down the food his body was desperately trying to expel.

When she finally appeared at his side, he jumped to his feet. "Bathroom!" he cried. "Where is the bathroom?"

The geisha, who spoke very little English, clearly did not understand the request. She shook her head and gestured with her hands, signaling she did not know what he was asking of her.

In that moment, Jacob lost the last bit of control he had over his stomach, and the food began to rise. Desperate to avoid vomiting on the floor right there at the head table, Jacob grabbed for the only receptacle he could find—the large, wide pocket on the front of his tunic. He jerked open the pocket and filled it with the contents of his upset stomach while his peers, the geisha, the emperor, the prime minister and five hundred other dignitaries looked on in horror.

The press, who had been invited to cover the event, leaped to their feet, and bathed poor Jacob in the blinding light of dozens of camera flashes, catching his most embarrassing moment on film. Utterly humiliated, Jacob allowed the emperor's staff to put him in a car and drive him back to the hotel where he could nurse his ailing stomach and his wounded pride in private. While Jacob recovered in his room, the Nigerian ambassador to Japan spent the evening begging and pleading with the press not to print the embarrassing photos of Jacob in the paper the next day. In the end, they agreed to keep the incident out of the media.

Jacob later discovered the dish he'd eaten was sushi, a Japanese delicacy that includes raw fish in its ingredients. Due to a mild allergy, seafood had never settled well with Jacob's stomach. After Jacob realized what he had eaten, he was not surprised by the outcome. Still, having a legitimate excuse for his unpleasant physical reaction did not eliminate the embarrassing aftereffects.

Jacob's friends arrived at the hotel later that evening and came to his room to tease him about the incident. For the next three months as the group toured various countries, Jacob endured their jibes and reminders about his weak stomach. "Don't throw up on anyone today," they joked. Because he later worked with many of these men in government positions, many years passed before they stopped teasing him.

After studying in Japan for one month, the group continued with their tour, visiting Russia, England, The United States and Austria. The Nigerians were scheduled to meet Gorbechev in Russia, but unexpected difficulties interfered. Unable to keep the appointment, Gorbechev cancelled the meeting. Similar difficulties arose in England, and their meeting with Margaret Thatcher was postponed, but foreign affairs officers took good care of the Nigerian visitors.

They also were scheduled to meet with the Queen of England, but because they missed their flight in New York, they didn't arrive in time to keep that appointment. However, Jacob would have an opportunity to meet her in later years.

* * *

As Jacob and Rose neared their 50s, God surprised them with an unexpected addition to their family. Since Timothy, their youngest son, had reached thirteen years of age, the Bawas assumed their childbearing years were behind them, but God saw fit to bless them with another daughter. They named their baby girl Lami (Thursday - feminine) Sophia Bawa. They dubbed her their retirement baby and thanked God for the blessing he'd chosen to give them late in life. The year following Lami's birth, the Bawa's oldest daughter Grace also gave birth to a daughter, whom she named Amena. So close in age, the two girls loved to play together and became close friends from an early age.

* * *

During the years Jacob served as Registrar of the Federal University of Technology and at the government's Ministries of Health and Education, Rose was teaching in a middle school. A teacher at heart, Jacob had never lost his desire to work with young people, and he and Rose dreamed of opening a school of their own to minister to the needs of children who wanted a more specialized education. Deciding to pursue that dream, Rose resigned from her teaching job and applied for a government grant to help begin a school.

The Bawas received a land grant and built a small school facility to house their educational program there in Minna. Rose started a program for kindergarten through fourth grade students.

14

Chapter Fourteen

Braving New Frontiers

In 1987, Jacob was attending an out-of-state meeting when he received a phone call from an excited friend. "Did you hear the announcement?" his friend asked.

Jacob had been busy with work and had no idea what announcement his friend was talking about. "What announcement?"

"The president has appointed you to be an ambassador!"

The news caught Jacob by surprise. "I have not heard anything about this."

Jacob and Rose sat in the living room of their quarters and turned on the television. Sure enough, Nigeria's president appeared in a news clip on the screen and said, "The following people have been appointed ambassadors...." Jacob's name was on the list.

Within several days the president's staff contacted Jacob to tell him he had been appointed to serve concurrently as ambassador to both Spain and the Vatican.

With no one qualified to run their primary school, Rose and Jacob were forced to close the facility. Though disappointed to see their efforts preempted, the Bawas knew the land and facilities would be there someday when they could return to resume the program. They wrapped up their personal affairs and closed the school.

Jacob's first tasks as ambassador took him to Lagos for orientation. There, he and Rose received protocol lessons and diplomacy training that would help them conduct themselves in a professional manner as they represented Nigeria's interests overseas. The orientation classes impressed upon Jacob that his actions as an ambassador could build foreign relationships or tear them down. Equipped with training, Jacob prepared to move his family to Europe to begin a new phase in his career.

• • •

Jacob, Rose, their children, and their elderly Aunt Apalu arrived in Spain in June 1987 and moved into a house the Nigerian government had purchased for its ambassadors. The residence, which sat in one of the richest neighborhoods of Madrid, was better described as a mansion.

Charles Bronson, an American film star, had built the home and lived there while doing some filming in Spain. When he sold the place, the Nigerian government purchased it for government use. The beautiful home had more than twelve bedrooms, which provided more than adequate accommodations for Jacob's large family. Each room was beautifully decorated and furnished in a style befitting a man of Jacob's position.

Amena, Jacob's granddaughter, was about nine months old when Jacob and Rose were preparing to leave for Spain. The infant suffered from severe medical problems and was not able to obtain the treatment she needed in Nigeria. Spain's medical facilities could possibly supply the needed treatment, so Grace and her husband began traveling back and forth between Nigeria and the Bawas' new residence in Spain. However, international travel soon became too costly for the young couple. Unable to afford the travel but desperate to see that their daughter received treatment, Grace and her husband placed the baby in Jacob and Rose's care. From that point on, Amena lived with her grandparents much of the time.

Eventually, she recovered from her childhood illness and grew into a strong young woman. Amena continued to spend much time with her grandparents and her aunt Lami, who had become her best friend and playmate.

• • •

Before Jacob could begin his ambassadorial service in Spain, he was required to go through the formality of meeting the king and presenting his credentials. On the day Jacob was appointed to meet King Carlos of Spain, a convoy arrived at his home to drive him to the palace. Jacob and

Rose were escorted to one of five luxury Rolls Royces near the middle of a long line of vehicles, which included police escorts, some of the king's staff, and other dignitaries.

Jacob learned visiting dignitaries usually rode in a carriage pulled by horses and paraded with much fanfare through the streets of the city. But a disease had plagued the horses of the city, so the king's thoroughbreds were being kept safely away from exposure. Even without a stately horse and carriage ride, the welcome the palace extended was impressive.

The lengthy convoy wound through the streets of Madrid and finally approached Palacio Real, the royal palace. They passed through the extensive gardens surrounding the palace, beautifully landscaped and adorned with statuary, fountains and stone walkways. As they neared their destination, the castle seemed to grow in size. Several stories high and sitting upon a foundation large enough to occupy several city blocks, it both impressed and intimidated Jacob. Row after row of stately columns and gilded windows lined the face of the massive building. The car slowed and parked at the edge of a large plaza leading up to the castle entrance.

An honor guard in colorful uniforms stood at attention before the entrance. When Jacob stepped out of his car, the honor guard began to play the Nigerian national anthem to welcome the newest ambassador to Spain. When the song ended, the commander of the guard stepped forward and instructed Jacob to inspect the honor guard, part of the ceremony involved in meeting the king.

About forty minutes later, Jacob followed his escort into the palace and walked through opulent hallways and rooms to the offices of King Carlos. The size and splendor of the royal palace impressed Jacob, who had never seen such a building before his trip to Spain. Marble floors, vaulted ceilings, and impressive artwork from some of the world's most recognized painters and sculptors adorned every room. He would have liked to linger in the halls to admire the décor, but his impending meeting with the king did not allow time for exploration.

The king's staff notified him of Jacob's arrival, and soon he emerged from an inner office to extend greetings. King Carlos looked regal in his formal attire with a blue sash draped across his chest, a red sash cinching his waist, and an array of medals pinned to his breast.

The president of Nigeria had given Jacob a letter of introduction, a scroll explaining Jacob credentials. It also included a letter assuring King

Carlos of the Nigerian government's support and confidence in Jacob's ability to serve as ambassador. Jacob presented the letter of introduction to King Carlos, and the two men sat down to get acquainted and discuss some key issues affecting their two countries.

After the private meeting, King Carlos and Jacob moved to a public room where Jacob was officially presented as the ambassador from Nigeria to Spain. The two men posed for pictures then Jacob and Rose returned home, riding in the Rolls Royce with the convoy in attendance.

• • •

While Jacob worked to establish himself in a new role, his family was also adapting to the change. Jerry, who had recently finished his secondary education, flew to the United States to attend a university. Timmy, still working on his high school studies, enrolled in an international school run by the British in Spain. Lami attended nursery school, allowing her busy parents to conduct their business during the day.

Rose assisted Jacob with his many duties—hosting guests, organizing parties, and filling in wherever a need arose. Nigeria's National Day always prompted a party at the Nigerian embassy, and extensive preparations for the affair began weeks in advance. Hors d'oeuvres, drinks, music, flowers, decorations—the parties were elaborate and expensive, but necessary. The ambassadors and other guests built relationships and cultivated business deals at the parties, so it was important to host and attend these galas.

Jacob frequently received invitations to attend similar parties at other embassies or at the palace. He received so many invitations, he grew weary of them. After spending long, hard days at work, Jacob often wished to stay home and rest rather than dressing up and attending another party. But as Nigeria's ambassador, he could not refuse an invitation to a party. To do so would insult the host and convey the impression that the relationship between the two countries was not cordial. So Jacob went, and Rose usually accompanied him.

The gatherings were usually held in large, open rooms where people could move freely. Guests stood for an hour or two, mingling with other ambassadors and heads of state. Rose's shoes would begin to pinch her feet, and Jacob, too, grew tired of standing. But their efforts reaped bountiful rewards. Through his work, Jacob helped to strengthen the relationship between Nigeria and Spain and found Spanish buyers for crude oil, one of Nigeria's chief exports.

• • •

During Jacob's service in Spain he had the opportunity to meet another famous member of a royal family: the Queen of England. She had come to the country for a state visit, and King Carlos invited Jacob and Rose, along with other ambassadors, to come to the palace to meet her. They arrived an hour prior to the scheduled appointment in order to participate in a protocol lesson. A protocol officer instructed them about the appropriate way to approach the queen, taught them how to address her properly, and explained other matters of etiquette. Rose learned to make a deep curtsy, and Jacob practiced bowing. After the lesson, each person scheduled to meet the queen was required to walk through a practice session to insure that the event would flow smoothly. When Queen Elizabeth arrived, Jacob and the other assembled guests walked through their choreographed greeting and met her.

• • •

Three months after beginning his role as ambassador to Spain, Jacob and Rose traveled to Rome, Italy. There, he scheduled a visit to the Vatican to present his credentials to Pope John Paul II and officially begin his service as ambassador to the Vatican.

As in Spain, a limousine arrived at the hotel to carry Jacob and Rose to their destination. They rode to the Vatican, a small city and technically a country unto itself, where they again inspected the honor guard that greeted them. Standing on either side of the basilica, the Vatican's Swiss guards, wearing Renaissance costumes with puffed sleeves and knickerbockers striped red, blue and yellow, made quite an impressive welcoming committee. After completing those formalities, the Vatican's Secretary of State escorted the Bawas to a private office and conducted another quick protocol lesson. Afterward, the pope was summoned, and Jacob was introduced.

Jacob presented his credentials to Pope John Paul II, and the pope asked Rose to wait in another office. He wished to speak with Jacob alone. Jacob was ushered into the pope's private chambers, and the staff brought two chairs and placed them in the center of the room. Jacob took the seat the Pope offered him. The two men sat knee to knee and conversed in English, a language they could both speak fluently. They discussed issues affecting Christians in Nigeria and other parts of the world, and each man shared his thoughts on the matter.

As Jacob stared into the pope's eyes, he could see the heartfelt sincerity and genuine concern with which he spoke. Here was a man who loved people and who cared deeply for God's children. Pope John Paul II's show of love and integrity impressed him greatly and Jacob knew he would enjoy working with the pope and the Vatican staff as he fulfilled his ambassadorial duties.

After the private meeting, Rose joined Jacob and the pope for a brief ceremony. Pope John Paul II stood before them and said, "God has given you a big responsibility. You are the light of the world. Take the name of Jesus with you wherever you go."

At the end of the ceremony, the pope presented Jacob and Rose with a small, white, wooden box.

"Open it," the pope instructed.

Jacob lifted the lid and found seven white candles nestled inside the box.

"Remember, you are the light of the world."

Jacob thanked the pope and left, encouraged and blessed by the meeting.

And so, Jacob began his diplomatic service to one of the world's most powerful and esteemed religious leaders.

• • •

After that day, Jacob served two ambassadorial roles concurrently, which meant he spent a great deal of time on airplanes flying between Spain and Italy to tend to his duties in both countries. The embassy staff had tickets ready for a moment's notice, and Jacob frequently used them.

He eventually acquired a residence in Italy, which he used during his extended visits to the Vatican. His family usually stayed in Spain while he traveled, since it was inconvenient to take the children out of school for weeks at a time.

As if serving two concurrent ambassadorships did not keep Jacob busy enough, he also served as Nigeria's Permanent Representative to the World Tourism Organization in Madrid, Spain. Each country of the world had representatives there to help promote and encourage international tourism. The job required a great deal of travel, so Jacob visited many countries around the world.

• • •

Jacob served as Nigeria's ambassador to the Vatican from 1987 to 1991. At the end of the term, the pope awarded Jacob the Distinguished Ambassadors Merit Award for his excellent service. The award is considered a great honor, similar to being knighted by a king. During an elaborate ceremony, the pope and his officials draped a sash across Jacob's shoulder and pinned a medal to his chest. They also presented Jacob with a silver, engraved plaque and translated the Latin inscription for him.

Unfortunately, years later someone broke into Jacob's home and stole these treasured gifts, so he no longer has them to remind him of his wonderful years of service to the pope.

• • •

In April 1991, the Nigerian government asked Jacob to serve as ambassador to the Republic of Chad, Nigeria's neighbor to the north. His service to the Vatican and Spain ended, and Jacob moved his family to Ndjamina, Chad. As in his previous ambassadorial positions, Jacob was required to present his credentials to President Idriss Deby, the President of Chad. The two men used a translator for their meeting, because while both men spoke several languages, the only one they had in common was Arabic. Jacob had learned Arabic in his primary school years but hadn't used it much since. To insure good communication, the men prudently decided to use a translator.

Chad had been ravaged by war for thirty years and desperately needed support in its efforts to rebuild. Jacob's mission was to help the country begin its recovery. While supplying aid was of great benefit to Chad, it also helped Nigeria, which had sheltered Chad's refugees who crossed the two countries' common border to escape the war.

"Tell me what you need," Jacob offered, "and the Nigerian government will do what it can to aid you."

"We desperately need vehicles," President Deby told Jacob.

"Is that all?"

"Years of war have depleted our assets in many areas. Obtaining vehicles is our primary concern, but of course, there is more."

"Make a list and together we will secure the resources you need."

Jacob tracked down five hundred new vehicles—mostly Pathfinders, and Jeeps—while President Deby and his staff assembled a list of other pressing needs.

• • •

Moving to Chad required some adjustments for Jacob and his family, one of which was adapting to the hotter climate. Chad is even hotter than Nigeria, and the country contains largely desert terrain. On average, the northern part of the country receives less than ten inches of rain a year, and the temperature climbs to one hundred thirty degrees on a regular basis. The south is more moderate but still much hotter and dryer than most countries. Jacob and his family found the heat oppressive at times. The temperatures were so high that if they put a bucket of water outdoors, within fifteen minutes, the water was too hot to touch.

The home the Nigerian embassy provided them was large and beautiful; however, it was also hard to cool. The three-floor residence had fifteen air conditioners, which ran nonstop, and yet the family still struggled to stay cool in the one hundred-plus temperatures.

As in Jacob's other ambassadorial positions, Rose served a vital role, assisting him in meeting the many demands of an ambassador's life. Lami, the only child remaining with them, attended an international school. She could not attend a Chadian school because classes were taught in French and Arabic. Though fluent in English, Spanish and several Nigerian languages, she could not speak the languages of Chad well enough to join the public schools.

Jacob's work with the Chadian government proved productive, strengthening the relationship between the two countries. In addition, Nigerian aid gave Chad the assistance they needed to strengthen their economy and rebuild a secure infrastructure, adding stability to the country and making them a strong neighbor and ally for Nigeria.

15

Chapter Fifteen

Returning Home

In 1993, Jacob returned to his home in Minna and requested retirement from his positions serving the Nigerian government. Government officials granted his request to leave his ambassadorship to Chad but tried to convince him to accept some other appointments, one of which involved serving as ambassador to Israel. Jacob politely refused every offer and insisted that he did not wish to continue in full-time government service.

Jacob's reasons for wanting to stay in Nigeria revolved around his family. He wanted Lami and Amena to learn the Nigerian languages and culture properly. They had spent much of their young lives traveling the world with him and had not spent as much time in their homeland as Jacob would have preferred. He did not want them to feel like strangers in their own country and so he decided to settle the family in Nigeria once again.

The government officials finally accepted Jacob's resolve and quit trying to place him in an overseas position. However, they did convince him to serve on the Police Community Relations Committee. This board helped to strengthen communication and dealings between the police force and the community, providing better protection and service for civilians. Accepting the part-time position seemed to satisfy the government and, at the same time, allowed Jacob time to pursue his other interests.

Jacob and Rose had plans to build a vocational school, and Jacob wanted to write some curriculum. For years he had entertained an interest in developing a program called Theological Education by Extension (T.E.E.), which would provide educational opportunities to pastors and church leaders who were actively ministering in Nigeria. Many pastors who wanted to continue their education were unable to leave their congregations to attend a Bible college. Through a program like T.E.E., lessons and curriculum could be sent through the mail. Once a month, a mentor or leader assigned by the school would meet with pastors to evaluate progress and offer guidance and instruction. In this way, many people who could never arrange for a traditional theological education could take classes by extension.

Seeing a great need for nontraditional educational programs, Jacob desired to develop curriculum and provide a means for working pastors and church leaders to enrich their theological education. Working only part-time with the Police Community Relations Committee allowed him plenty of time to study, do research and write curriculum.

• • •

Jacob sat in his favorite chair scribbling notes on a pad of paper when the shrill ring of the telephone pierced the tranquil peace of his study time. Rose moved to answer it, but Jacob held up his hand to stop her. "Don't answer it, please. I've had five calls in the last hour. I'm not getting any work done with so many interruptions."

After just one year in Nigeria, Jacob admitted that if he wanted to do some serious writing, he would have to leave the country. His telephone rang continually with job offers, social invitations, speaking engagements and other matters that drew him away from his project. He realized that as long as he remained in the country, he would be too busy to write the curriculum. So in 1994, he left Nigeria in part to escape his popularity. He came to the United States, intending to take a teaching position at a Christian university.

He had hoped the Fort Wayne Bible Institute in Indiana would have a place for him because he knew they had an extensive library, which would provide him with excellent resources as he wrote his curriculum. But when he called John Moran, who now served as a pastor in Indiana, Jacob discovered the Bible college in Fort Wayne had been merged with another college. John Moran suggested Jacob apply at one of his alma maters, Bethel College, in Mishawaka, Indiana.

Jacob had not had contact with the school's leadership since his graduation several decades earlier and figured that many of the people he knew from the school had moved to other jobs or retired. He asked John to put him in touch with the right people. John made a few calls, and subsequently the school's president, Dr. Norman Bridges, invited Jacob to join Bethel's teaching staff.

When Jacob accepted the position, he made it clear that he intended to stay only a couple semesters. "Give me the title Visiting Professor because I am staying only one year," Jacob suggested.

College administrators agreed, and Jacob moved to the United States, bringing Rose, Lami and Amena with him. The girls enrolled in the local school system, while Rose worked part-time as a nurse's assistant. Jacob settled into a routine of teaching, studying, and writing, thankful to be making progress on his T.E.E. curriculum after decades of dreaming of developing such a program.

• • •

Shortly after settling in, Jacob discovered a wonderful perk that came from living in Mishawaka. Many of the missionaries who had impacted his life throughout the years—Naomi Everett, Art and Gladys Reifel, Mrs. Russell Sloat, and Jacob's good friend, John Moran who was serving as President of the Missionary Church, Inc.—lived within an hour's drive of the Bethel campus. These missionaries, who had served as his spiritual mothers, fathers, and mentors, had retired and returned to their homes in northern Indiana.

Whenever they were able, the group gathered to eat, fellowship, reminisce about their missionary days and discuss current issues affecting Nigeria. Rose always cooked a Nigerian dish to bring to the dinner—usually bean cakes, which were a favorite among the group. They also saw one another each year at general conference and stole away for a few hours to visit. Years of serving together in the mission field had forged a special bond among them, and they thanked God for bringing them together to enjoy one another's company again.

• • •

Jacob's first year at Bethel brought with it honor and recognition from the school's administration and his fellow alumni. In 1994, he became the recipient of the Alumnus of the Year Award. During the Homecoming weekend, a time when many alumni return to Bethel to fellowship with one another and honor alumni who have achieved accomplishments worthy of recognition, several hundred Bethel graduates gathered in the college Dining Commons for brunch and a special ceremony.

Jacob and Rose, along with their daughter and granddaughter, attended the function. After enjoying a brunch buffet, the program commenced with a musical number. When the time came to present the award, Jacob's former teacher and friend, Naomi Everett, introduced Jacob, sharing stories about his youth and bragging about his accomplishments. With a smile gracing her lips and pride glowing from her face, she called him forward to receive the award.

When Jacob took the podium, he expressed his gratitude for having had the opportunity to attend Bethel and for the impact the college had on his life.

• • •

As Jacob's first year at Bethel came to an end, he faced a big decision. His curriculum was not finished, and his family was just settling into a comfortable routine in the States. In addition, he loved teaching at Bethel and enjoyed being a part of the close-knit college community. Perhaps he had been overly optimistic when he insisted on staying only one year. When Jacob expressed an interest in staying another year, Bethel's administrators extended him an open invitation to stay and teach as long as he liked.

Jacob decided to prolong his stay and purchased a home conveniently located several blocks from the college. His sons, James, Jerry and Timmy, came to spend time with their parents in the United States and to attend Bethel College. The arrangement proved beneficial to the family and the college, so Jacob decided to stay until God prompted him otherwise.

During Dr. Bawa's nine-year stay at Bethel, he taught many different subjects. Having such a varied background and extensive education, Dr. Bawa was an asset to several departments at Bethel College. Using his degree in Theology, he taught courses on religion, philosophy and Old and New Testament studies. In the Education Department, he taught classes on multicultural education techniques, middle school education, and how to develop curriculum. His heritage and life experiences made Jacob an ideal teacher for geography classes like sub-Saharan Africa or

Africa and the Middle East. He also served as an academic advisor to students majoring in international relations or preparing to work in the field of missions.

Outside the classroom, Jacob remained active in pulpit ministry. He traveled across the United States, speaking and teaching at churches, conferences, and seminars. His efforts helped raise awareness about missionary programs in Nigeria and the spiritual needs in that country.

• • •

For Jacob, 1996 proved to be an active year, full of opportunities and honors. While in the United States, Jacob continued to receive job offers from his government. Changes at the United Nations prompted the election of a new Secretary General. Nigeria was afforded the opportunity to nominate a candidate for the position, and governmental officials immediately thought of Jacob.

The president of Nigeria phoned Jacob to offer him the nomination to serve as Secretary General of the United Nations. Not interested in returning to diplomatic service, Jacob quietly declined the offer. He continued teaching and working on his curriculum, feeling he could serve God's greater purpose in continuing on his current course.

In April 1996, board members of the Honor Society of The Association of Canadian Bible Colleges telephoned Jacob. "Would you be able to attend commencement ceremonies at Emmanuel Bible College? We want to present you with an award."

Jacob cleared his schedule, and he and Rose traveled to Kitchener, Ontario. Before the graduating class, their family and friends, in addition to many alumni and invited guests, the Honor Society presented Jacob with an award for his outstanding achievements in ministry, diplomacy, and education.

As summer drew near, Jacob and Rose began preparations for a trip overseas. The liberal arts program at Bethel College encourages students to study abroad, taking missions trips to foreign countries for both experience and college credits. Dr. Bawa had agreed to organize and mentor a missionary trip to Ghana, which took place immediately after classes ended in May.

The thirty students and faculty arrived at the airport in Accra, Ghana's capital city, weary from the lengthy flight. While passing through customs, officials found a problem with one student's passport. It appeared they might not be allowed through, but Dr. Bawa stepped forward and introduced himself. The students watched in fascination as the customs officers' attitudes changed. Moments before the group had been treated like pesky tourists, but now they were given preferential treatment. Students had heard stories of Dr. Bawa's accomplishments and the respect in which he is held overseas, but they had never seen him in such a role. The experience left them more aware of the honor and respect Dr. Bawa had earned through his years of distinguished service.

Outside the airport, the group from Bethel boarded a police bus, which would serve as their primary transportation throughout the three-week trip. The bus drove them to a hotel where they stayed for the next week. Each morning, the police bus arrived at their lodgings and drove them to a location on the outskirts of the city. The group filed out of the bus and searched out an open area suitable for ministry. Students began their impromptu, street-side services by singing. The music drew attention, and soon a crowd gathered around to listen. After the music, students ministered through skits and dramas with messages intended to pull at the hearts of bystanders. Then Dr. Bawa stepped forward and delivered a message in both Hausa and English, inviting the people to come and experience the blessings of living for Christ.

The trip impacted the hearts of Ghana's people, and many accepted Christ as their Savior. The trip also left a deep impression on the students. After a week in Accra, the group moved on to visit Cape Coast and several smaller cities in between. Their evangelistic efforts and results were much the same in each city.

While the group worked hard at their evangelistic efforts, Dr. Bawa also allowed them some time for fun and relaxation. On one day, they toured a former slave trading post and several other locations with historical significance. While in Cape Coast they visited the beautiful coastline and lay on the beaches in the afternoons. At the end of the three-week trip, the group flew home, changed by their experiences.

16

Chapter Sixteen

Homecoming

The year 2003 arrived and Jacob sensed that God was leading him to return home to Nigeria. He had spent nine wonderful years in northern Indiana, teaching, writing, and enjoying the fellowship of the missionaries who had played such a vital role in his early years. Perhaps the only drawback was the winter snow and frigid temperatures that he still found disagreeable. Yet, his dream to begin a theological education by extension program still burned in his heart. In addition, he and Rose still owned the property and facilities for their school in Minna, and God had given them vision for how to use it.

In recent years, Nigerian cities have experienced an influx of young people looking for jobs. But without proper training or work experience, all too many of these young people find themselves without prospects. The lack of employment and loss of hope leads to drug use, alcohol addiction and criminal activity for many.

Responding to the need, Jacob and Rose Bawa began laying groundwork to open the Memorial Vocational Training School, providing vocational training programs for high school graduates in a Christian-based environment. The goal is to help students become productive, self-sufficient citizens. The school offers professional certificates and training in computer science, carpentry, office management, auto mechanics, administrative assistant/secretarial, bookkeeping, tailoring, home economics, furniture and cabinet making, agriculture, plumbing, electronics and masonry. Armed with practical skills and the Word of God, the students will leave the school to become competent, professional citizens.

Jacob and Rose discussed the matter and agreed: the time had come for them to pursue this dream. They decided Jacob should finish teaching the spring semester, then use the quiet summer months to make the extensive arrangements necessary to transport their household and lives overseas. Jacob spoke with school administrators expressing his intention to leave in the summer. While they were disappointed to lose an excellent teacher, they believed in Jacob's vision for the trade school and T.E.E. program.

"We'd like to offer you whatever assistance we can. Maybe we could begin by setting up a fund to collect donations and raise financial support for your project," administrators offered. Grateful for the enthusiastic show of support, Jacob agreed. With the college's blessing, he began preparations to move.

• • •

Jacob sat in his living room one afternoon in May, doing the final editing on the last few sections of his curriculum. The college semester was nearly complete, and he and Rose had settled on a date of departure. They hoped to return to Nigeria at the beginning of August, giving them about two months to wrap up their affairs. Just a week earlier, Jacob had called a realtor and put their house on the market, hoping to close on the sale prior to their departure.

Rose entered the room, the car keys in her hand and her purse hanging from her arm. "I'm going to pick the girls up from school."

Jacob glanced her way. "They aren't coming home on the bus?"

"No. They had an after-school activity today. I might stop at the store while I'm out. Do you need anything?"

Jacob shook his head. "No, thank you. I'm going to try to finish this work." He tapped the stack of papers on his lap.

Rose nodded and headed toward the door. "I'll be back in a little while."

The door closed behind her, and Jacob heard the car purr to life and drive away. He returned his attention to his work, enjoying a cup of coffee as he scratched notes in the margins. Soon, he lifted his coffee cup to his lips and realized it was empty. Sighing, he set his papers aside, pushed to his feet and carried his cup to the kitchen.

Normally, Rose would be in the kitchen at this hour, preparing an after-school snack for the girls. The kitchen seemed unnaturally quiet in her absence. Jacob set his cup on the countertop, lifted the coffee pot and filled his cup. He pulled the sugar bowl toward him only to realize he had left his stirring spoon on the end table beside his chair. He retraced his steps to the living room and found the spoon where he had left it.

As he turned to go back into the kitchen, an earsplitting crack ripped through his home. His kitchen cupboards exploded into the center of the room, their contents shooting out and crashing to the floor. The microwave resting on his counter flew toward him, missing Jacob's shoulder by inches. The kitchen wall crumbled and everything connected to it tumbled to the floor.

When the dust and debris began to settle, Jacob could see the hood of a car poking through the wreckage of his kitchen. Someone had driven her car into the side of his home! Had Rose been in the kitchen preparing a snack, or if he had not walked to his chair to find the spoon, either of them could have been seriously hurt. God had protected them from harm. He rushed outside to see if the driver had been injured. An elderly woman sat at the wheel, looking dazed and upset but not seriously injured. Within minutes, emergency crews arrived to assist them.

Several hours later, the driver had been taken to the hospital for a checkup and the car removed from Jacob's property. The emergency crews had done all they could to help, but Jacob was left to cope with a tremendous amount of damage. One look at the gaping hole in his kitchen wall and Jacob knew they could not live in the house until they made some repairs. Plumbing and electrical systems had been damaged, and he had no way to seal the house from the elements or intruders. He called the insurance company to discuss the matter, and they suggested he take his family to a hotel until the situation could be remedied.

As the family gathered some clothing and personal belongings, another disheartening reality dawned on Jacob. He was due to leave the country in several months and needed to sell his home. But no one was going to buy the home until the damage could be repaired. Did he have time to repair the damage, find a buyer and close before August? Not likely. If he hoped to open his school by the January term, he could not afford to delay his return to Nigeria. With questions weighing heavily on his mind, he and his family put their luggage in the car and drove to a hotel.

Initially, hotel living seemed a luxury, but the family quickly tired of it. They spent too much time in a cramped room and ate all their meals at restaurants. They missed their own beds and longed for some home-cooked meals.

Several weeks passed, and Jacob made little progress on his home repairs. Contractors already had full summer schedules and couldn't fit him in, even though his situation was an emergency. He had managed to clear the worst of the debris and temporarily seal the hole, but the renovation could not be completed before he left the country. Searching for a solution, Jacob approached some trusted friends and explained his dilemma.

"We'd be happy to help you," they offered. "You go ahead and leave as scheduled. We will make sure the renovations are completed and will oversee the sale of your home."

Relief flooded through Jacob. He would trust God and his friends to work out the details on his behalf. With that concern settled, Jacob refocused his attention on the moving plans.

• • •

In the weeks prior to their departure, the Bawas attended many banquets, services and gatherings held in their honor. Friends, colleagues and church congregations wanted to say goodbye to a family that had blessed them during the past nine years. One of the more poignant goodbyes happened on a Thursday evening in the fellowship hall of Bethany Missionary Church in Osceola, Indiana. The missionaries who knew Jacob from his youth gathered for one last Nigerian party, each bringing a dish and many happy memories to share. Naomi Everett, the Reifels, Mrs. Russell Sloat, and around twenty others had come to wish him well.

Jacob, Rose and their girls were greeted with smiles and hugs. The women set out the food, and the meal began amidst much joyful reminiscing. After the plates were cleared, Jacob stood at the front of the hall and spoke. He regaled his friends with a comical tale of a car destroying his house, able to laugh about the incident now that several weeks had passed. When the laughter died down, he grew serious. "You have been my spiritual mothers and fathers," he said, looking deep into the eyes of the men and women who had impacted his life. "You sacrificed so much to come to my country and my village to tell people like me about Jesus Christ. I would not be what I am today if not for your obedience to God. I cannot thank you enough for all you've done for me."

In response, the missionaries' faces glowed with love and parental pride. "We couldn't be more proud of you if you were our own son," one of the ladies told him. The others nodded their agreement.

"Sing us a song in Hausa," someone suggested. "Sing 'Jesus Loves Me'."

Jacob drew a breath and sang the first line of the song. The missionaries joined in, and soon the room filled with voices lifted in song. They sang and shared for another hour before ending the evening in prayer.

Saying goodbye to the many friends they had made during their years in Indiana was difficult, but at the same time, they looked forward to seeing their home and countrymen again. In August 2003, Jacob, Rose, Lami and Amena said goodbye to Mishawaka, their home of nine years, and boarded an intercontinental flight which carried them to their homeland.

The Missionary Church is an evangelical denomination with head-
quarters in Fort Wayne, Indiana. It is also associated with the
Evangelical Missionary Church of Canada and the United Missionary
Church of Nigeria. At the time Jacob was growing to manhood, these
churches operated as the United Missionary Society in Nigeria.
Bethel College is a Christian liberal arts college of some 2,000 stu-
dents. It is located in Mishawaka, Indiana and is the college of the
Missionary Church.
Persons wishing to support the ministry of Dr. Jacob and Rose Bawa
are invited to contact Dr. Dennis Engbrecht, Senior Vice President,
Bethel College, 1001 W. McKinley Ave., Mishawaka, IN 46545, or send
donations to the address below.
Bethel College Institutional Advancement Dept.
on behalf of Dr. Jacob Bawa
1001 W. McKinley Ave.
Mishawaka, IN 46545-5591

Please make checks payable to Bethel College and note Dr. Bawa's
name on the memo line of your check. Thank you.

Timeline

January 1958 – December 1958 . . . . .Teacher/Headmaster,
U.M.S. Primary School Salka, Nigeria

January 1959 – December 1959 . . . . . .Teacher, Rural Education Center, Minna, Nigeria

January 1963 – July 1966 . . . . .Principal, Hausa Bible School, Salka, Nigeria

January 1963 – July 1966 . . . . .Minister, Salka United Missionary Church

July 1967 – July 1969 . . . . .Lecturer, Ilorin Theological Seminary

July 1967 – July 1969 . . . . .Lecturer, Government Teachers' College, Ilorin, Nigeria

July 1967 – December 1969 . .Manager, Chapel Nursery/Primary School, Ilorin, Nigeria

January 1973 – August 1975 . . . . .Principal, Ilorin Theological Seminary

January 1973 – August 1975 . . . . . .Minister, Ilorin Theological College Chapel, Nigeria

January 1976 – June 1979 . . . . .Graduate Assistant, Michigan State University;
Dept. of Oriental and African Studies

July 1979 – October 1979 . . . . .Instructor, Michigan State University;
Dept. of Oriental and African Studies

January 1978   January 1979 . . . . .Director of Personnel Department,
TED Welding Company, Lansing, MI

January 1979 – January 1980 . . . . .President, Missionary Church of Nigeria

March 1980 – March 1981 . . . . .Chief Inspector of Education,
Niger State Ministry of Education

January 1982 – January 1983 . . . . .National Teachers' Institute, Board Member

January 1982 – December 1983 . . . . .Permanent Secretary, Ministry of Education,
Niger State

January 1984 – December 1986 . . . . .Director, United Bank of Africa

January 1984 – May 1987 . .Registrar, Federal University of Technology, Minna, Nigeria

January 1985 – May 1987 . . .Chairman, Niger State Scholarship Board, Minna, Nigeria

June 1987 – April 1991 . . . . .Nigerian Ambassador to Spain

June 1987 – April 1991 . . . . .Nigerian Ambassador to the Vatican

June 1987 – April 1991 . . . . .Nigeria's Permanent Representative to
World Tourism Organization

April 1991 – March 1993 . . . . .Nigerian Ambassador to the Republic of Chad

August 1994 – to June 2003 . . . .Visiting Professor, Bethel College, Mishawaka, Indiana

Degrees

Michigan State University, East Lansing, Michigan
Ph.D. Curriculum & Instruction

Michigan State University, East Lansing, Michigan
M.A. Education

Trinity International University, Deerfield, Illinois
M.A. Christian Education (Cum Laude)

Bethel College, Mishawaka, Indiana
Certificate in General Studies

Emmanuel Bible College, Kitchener, Ontario, Canada
B.Th. Biblical Literature

Ilorin Theological Seminary (affiliate of University of Ibadan, Nigeria)
Diploma in Theology

Acknowledgements

A book such as this one would not have been possible without the contributions and cooperation of many wonderful people. My heartfelt thanks goes to all who so graciously gave of themselves and their memories:

Dr. Jacob Bawa—who sat through hours of endless questions, patiently taught me about Nigeria, and blessed me with the story of his life. I have learned so much from you, and because of our interaction, I am changed forever.

Dr. Norman Bridges—whose heart and vision for this project precipitated the writing of this book.

Professor Kim Peterson—who oversaw this writing project, offering direction, encouragement and editorial input. Your contributions were invaluable.

Dr. Christian Davis—who contributed a valuable critique and advice during the editing process.

Rev. Art & Gladys Reifel—who educated me about Salka, Nigeria, and provided countless resources which added so much to this book.

Naomi Everett—for her wonderful recollections of Jacob's days at U.M.S., Zuru, and for the many hours she spent on the phone patiently answering my questions.

Dr. John Moran—for telling me about Jacob's first baptism and sharing stories of their service together in Salka and their friendship which has lasted for decades.

Mrs. Russell Sloat—who contributed details about her husband's service as Principal of Ilorin Theological Seminary and their association with Jacob.

Dr. Dennis Engbrecht—who searched Bethel's files and provided me with names of potential interviewees.

Rev. Don Granitz—long-time friend of Jacob who read the manuscript and offered feedback.

Eon Johnson—who shared his memories of the missionary trip to Ghana.

And most of all, thanks be to God, the Author and Finisher of our faith.